CLASSICAL SURVIVALS

CLASSICAL SURVIVALS

The Classics in the Modern World

Hugh Lloyd-Jones
Regius Professor of Greek
in the University of Oxford

Duckworth

First published in 1982 by
Gerald Duckworth & Co. Ltd
The Old Piano Factory
43 Gloucester Crescent, London NW1
Second impression 1988

ISBN 0 7156 1517 3 (cased)

British Library Cataloguing in Publication Data

Lloyd-Jones, Hugh
    Classical survivals: the
    classics in the modern world.
    1. Civilization, Greek 2. Rome
    Civilization
    I. Title
    938   DE71

    ISBN 0-7156-1517-3

Photoset by E.B. Photosetting Ltd
Woodend Avenue, Speke, Liverpool
and printed in Great Britain by
Bookcraft (Bath) Ltd.

'In dealing with Greek literature, as with every other, in order to understand we must also feel.'

Gilbert Murray, Inaugural Lecture, 1909

'If we carefully control every statement we make about an ancient theory or belief by reference to the evidence, if we are constantly on the watch against importing Christian or other modern preconceptions into antiquity, it seems to me that we have a slender chance of getting at the truth. Most likely we shall fail; at best, we may get at that fraction of the truth which it is possible for our generation to apprehend.'

Hugh Lloyd-Jones, Inaugural Lecture, 1961

Contents

Preface

Most of the essays published in this collection are book reviews; with few exceptions they have appeared in the English weekly papers, principally *The Times Literary Supplement* and the *Spectator*. No. 9 was originally a letter to the Editor of the *Spectator*, No. 27 was the introduction to a volume of selections from Tacitus, and No. 28 was a lecture given at Delphi.

The book does not pretend to be a contribution to scholarship; as a colleague the other day remarked, I often review books about which I do not claim to be an expert. That is natural, for reviewing for the weekly papers is a kind of writing with its own laws, and these essays are addressed not to specialists, but to the educated general public.

I thank all who have given permission to reprint, and particularly the two editors for whom most of my reviews have been written. I started reviewing for the weeklies in the fifties, when Professor Karl Miller was Literary Editor of the *Spectator*. Like many other contributors to *The Times Literary Supplement*, I owe a special debt to Mr John Gross, who has made that periodical better than it ever was. I also thank Professor Mary Lefkowitz and Mr Colin Haycraft for their invaluable help.

Oxford, 1982   H.Ll.-J.

1

Mediaeval and Humanistic Greek

At the time of his lamented death, at sixty-three, in 1969, Roberto Weiss was planning a collection of those among his essays which bore on the question of the knowledge of Greek in western Europe during the Middle Ages, particularly the later Middle Ages and the early Renaissance. The material he had collected was passed by his widow to his London colleagues, who now publish it, together with a list of the author's publications and two good indexes. Fourteen of the essays are in Italian, five in English; two of the former, on the history of Greek studies at the Papal Curia during the late thirteenth and the fourteenth centuries and on the study of Greek in Florence, have not appeared before.

There is no point in complaining that Weiss did not work the material together into a single book, thus eliminating repetition; the writing is so clear and the arrangement so sensible that the essays make excellent reading, and the repetition helps the reader to grasp essential facts. Weiss in his preface abjures the intention of offering a complete study of the subject, even for the period between the end of the thirteenth and the beginning of the fifteenth century. He has concentrated on certain important centres, omitting France (except for Paris and St Denis), Italy (except for the Papal Curia and the territory south of Naples), the Low Countries and the imperial domains; and he offers no general treatment of the principal religious orders. None the less the book's contents make a very great contribution to the subject. The author shows an impressive mastery of detail, and clearly states his main conclusion, that such interest in Greek as there was in the West during this period was purely practical. People who studied Greek at all studied it for the sake of theology, philosophy or science, particularly medical science, not for the sake of history or of literature.

From an early date the two halves of the Roman Empire showed a

* A review of *Medieval and Humanistic Greek* by Roberto Weiss in *The Times Literary Supplement*, 3 February 1978.

strong tendency to split apart. About half the Greek world supported
Mithridates of Pontus in his revolt against Rome; half a century later,
more than half of it supported Antony and Cleopatra against
Augustus. Under Constantine the Romans were forced to divide the
empire into two halves. The decline of Greek studies in the western
half was alarmingly rapid. Even a well-educated provincial who went
to Italy to complete his education, like St Augustine (d. 430) could
remain ignorant of Greek; his contemporaries depended on
translators like Jerome and Rufinus for their knowledge of the
Christian writings of the Greek-speaking East. The fall of the western
empire during the fifth century did not improve the situation, and the
temporary reconquest of Italy by Justinian during the sixth did not
retrieve it. Translation of secular authors was rare; Calcidius's fourth-
century version of the *Timaeus* was for 800 years the only Latin
translation of a Platonic dialogue, and Boethius's grand design of a
series of translations of Plato and Aristotle was interrupted by his
execution. Cassiodorus's library at Vivarium contained some Greek
books, and he himself tried to encourage translation. But there was
little interest in Greek during the early Middle Ages.

Charlemagne had diplomatic relations with the court of
Constantinople, and later the Byzantine princess Theophano became
the wife of Otto II and mother of Otto III. But the ninth-century
conflict between Pope Nicholas I and the Patriarch Photius imported
a fatal element of *odium theologicum* into relations between East and
West. Later Venetian and Genoese relations with the East developed
rapidly, and the Crusades brought East and West into a closer
contact. But neither merchants nor crusaders, and still less priests,
proved good cultural ambassadors. In 1204 the hostility reached its
peak with the sack of Constantinople by the Crusaders under
Venetian leadership. Despite all the efforts later made to promote a
reconciliation between the two churches, culminating with the
Council of Florence in the fifteenth century that was, in theory only
and too late, successful, each in the last resort preferred the Muslim
infidel to the other. It is an irony of our own time that this fact, one of
the saddest in European history, should now seem one of the most
encouraging which history contains, since it nourishes the hope that
the Communist Churches of Russia and China may prove Christian
in their refusal to be reconciled.

There was, however, one part of western Europe which throughout
the Middle Ages belonged culturally, though not politically, to the
Byzantine sphere. Sicily remained Byzantine till the Arab conquest of
the ninth century; Calabria, Lucania and Apulia till the Norman
conquest of the eleventh. In Sicily the Norman rulers after an initial

period of hostility established good relations with their Greek subjects. The Greeks were still more favoured by the Hohenstaufens. Frederick II is said to have known Greek. The twelfth century saw a revival of interest in ancient Greek writings; interested in Greek philosophy through the Arabic translations, Sicilian scholars had access to Greek sources also. Henry Aristippus, archdeacon of Catania, who died in 1162, translated Plato's *Phaedo* and *Meno*, parts of Aristotle, and the treatise on engineering of Hero of Byzantium. Adelard of Bath, visiting Sicily at this time, helped the famous Admiral Eugenius of Palermo to make a Latin version of the *Almagest*; John of Salisbury learnt Greek from an inhabitant of Sta. Severina. The Patirion monastery of Rossano had theological books, but the monastery of St Nicholas at Casola had even literary texts, and its monks continued to make copies. Quintus of Smyrna was once called 'Quintus Calaber' because his main manuscript was here; so was that of Coluthus' *Rape of Helen* and, in all probability, the famous Ravenna manuscript of Aristophanes.

The Angevin monarchs, creatures of the Papacy, could not be expected to treat the Greeks with the same sympathy as their Hohenstaufen predecessors. But even they encouraged the work of translation, especially that of scientific books; Robert I was interested in medicine, and promoted versions of Galen and of certain Hippocratic works. Sicilian poets turned out Greek verses no worse than those of their contemporaries in Constantinople. The Greek rite was observed in some parts of Sicily till the sixteenth century, and Weiss tells us that Greek is still spoken in Bova and other inaccessible places, just as it was when Norman Douglas was in Calabria.

A link with Sicily and Magna Graecia seems to have made possible what Weiss calls 'that wonderful rise of Greek studies which took place in thirteenth-century England'. During the first half of the century it centred upon Robert Grosseteste, Bishop of Lincoln and Chancellor of Oxford University (d. 1253). His version of the popular work of 'Dionysius the Areopagite' (of which more presently) on the names of God contained an introduction to Greek grammar: in 1958 there was discovered in the Bodleian a manuscript of Aristotle evidently copied at Grosseteste's order by a scribe ignorant of Greek. One of his assistants, Nicholas the Greek, had come from Sicily; another, John of Basingstoke, had learnt Greek in Athens from Constantina, daughter of the Archbishop of the place. Some survivors of this circle may have been in touch with Roger Bacon, who attached great importance to the diffusion of an accurate knowledge of Greek, together with Hebrew, Arabic and Syriac.

Bacon severely criticised existing translations, and wrote a Greek grammar markedly different from that produced in Grosseteste's circle. Several copies of this work made during the two following centuries exist in England; but here as on the Continent the study of Greek lost ground during the fourteenth century. After 1295 no work of Aristotle was translated before Leonardo Bruni in the early fifteenth century. But as the old tradition of Greek studies died, a new one with very different motives was beginning to arise in Italy.

The Carolingian contacts with Byzantium had one startling consequence for Greek studies. In 827 the envoys of Michael the Stammerer presented Louis le Pieux with a magnificent uncial codex of the works of the so-called Dionysius the Areopagite, that writer who during the fifth or early sixth century put out under the name of St Paul's Athenian convert a synthesis of Christian and neo-Platonic theology. The king handed this over to the monks of St Denis, who were as glad to have their patron's writings as they would have been to have his jawbone. One of their number, Hilduin, produced a translation; one wonders whether the donors of the manuscript had supplied a teacher. During the next generation this was revised by the most distinguished member of the monastery, John Scotus Eriugena; presumably he learnt Greek in the monastery itself. During the twelfth century, when interest in philosophy had spread widely, we find first a scholar in close touch with the monks and then one of their own number actually travelling to Greece and Constantinople to get new manuscripts of Dionysius, which were used in making a new translation. In 1167 their learned abbot taught a little Greek to Herbert of Bosham, the secretary and biographer of Thomas Becket. The Emperor Manuel Palaeologus during his visit to France in 1400 made contact with the monks; so did George Hermonymus, who began teaching Greek to French humanists in 1476.

Despite the tradition of Greek learning at St Denis, there is no evidence that Greek was taught in the Sorbonne before the thirteenth century. David of Dinant, whose pantheistic doctrine was condemned in 1210, knew Greek, but we do not know whether he taught in Paris. But some translations of Aristotle were made there. William de Mara, an English Franciscan associated with Roger Bacon, spent most of his life there; so did the Flemish Franciscan Gerard de Huy, who in his *Liber Triglossus* offered a grammar of the three biblical languages.

Greek books naturally existed at the Papal Curia, which acquired the Greek library of the Hohenstaufens by gift from the conqueror of Manfred, Charles of Anjou, in 1266. During the second half of the thirteenth century, St Thomas Aquinas set out to adapt the philosophy of Aristotle to the requirements of the Church. He was acquainted with the St Denis translation of Dionysius, and himself wrote a commentary on his treatise on the names of God; this accounts for a decided neo-Platonic bias in the saint's interpretation of Aristotle. His friend the Flemish Dominican William de Moerbeke, working in Rome, meanwhile provided systematic translations of a very large number of Aristotle's works. Apart from their importance for medieval culture, these were made by a method which makes it possible to reconstruct Greek manuscripts used by de Moerbeke which are now lost, and their publication in modern times has done scholars a very notable service.

The negotiations for the union of the churches that began in 1261 made it desirable for the Curia to command the services of persons who knew Greek. At the end of the century Raymond Lull campaigned actively for Greek, Arabic and Hebrew to be studied, and in 1312 the Council of Vienne decreed that chairs of Greek and Oriental languages should be set up at Bologna, Paris, Oxford and Salamanca. But the decree remained a dead letter; the union of the churches was not attained, and the Aristotelian tradition was beginning to decline.

One of the Byzantine prelates whom the negotiations brought to the papal court at Avignon was Barlaam of Calabria, who between 1339 and 1342 gave a few lessons in Greek to Petrarch. Now for the first time – with the possible exception of the astonishing Richard de Bury, Bishop of Durham and author of the *Philobiblon* – we find someone setting out to learn Greek not for theological or practical but for humanistic motives. It was indeed impossible for anyone as steeped in Latin literature and as devoted to it as Petrarch was to remain unaware of the importance of Greek literature, which Cicero and Virgil so explicitly attest. But when Rudolf Pfeiffer writes that 'everyone could feel how ardently he longed to know the Greek background of Roman literature', Weiss provides a salutary corrective. He points out that Petrarch was not exempt from the contempt for Greece often expressed by Roman chauvinism and strongly encouraged by Catholic prejudice against the Eastern Church; and he reminds us that after Barlaam's departure to the see of Gerace in 1342, Petrarch could quite well have continued his Greek lessons with Simon Atumanus, the Byzantine cleric who brought the Laurentian manuscript of the alphabetic plays of Euripides to the West. In 1354 Petrarch was given a copy of the *Iliad* by Nicholas Sigeros, the envoy of the Byzantine emperor to the papal court; but during the twenty years of life still left to him he never learnt to read it.

Boccaccio, on the other hand, picked up a little Greek from Leontius Pilatus, the Calabrian who at Florence between 1360 and 1362 was the first person officially employed to teach Greek in any western centre. His Latin translations from Homer, feeble as they were, were epoch-making. At the turn of the century, better translations came from the circle of Coluccio Salutati, who in 1397 brought the Byzantine Manuel Carysoloras to teach in Florence. Salutati's younger friend Iacopo Angeli di Scarperia, who translated works by Plutarch and Ptolemy, was the first Italian humanist to visit Constantinople in order to learn Greek and perhaps the first of his generation to collect Greek manuscripts. But translators like him and Roberto Rossi, who made a version of the *Posterior Analytics* of Aristotle, were soon eclipsed by the achievements of Leonardo Bruni, whose versions of Plutarch, Xenophon, Plato and Aristotle initiated a new phase in Greek studies.

2

Classical Scholarship 1300-1850

Hitler did more for classical studies in this country than for most branches of education. To draw an analogy from a different discipline, it was as though the leading members of one of the greatest Australian elevens had quarrelled with the Board of Control and qualified to play for England. None of the famous scholars who came here from Germany at that time was more eminent than Rudolf Pfeiffer. Born in 1889 at Augsburg, in Bavaria, he grew up in the house whose walls the sixteenth-century humanist Conrad Peutinger had decorated with maps; and he received his early education at the Benedictine school of St Stephen under its celebrated headmaster, Dom Beda Grundl. At the University of Munich he studied under Otto Crusius, the biographer of Rohde and, like him, as cultivated as he was learned. Later he moved to Berlin, and profited from the very different teaching of Wilamowitz, but he never departed from the typically South German and Catholic traditions in which he had grown up.

In Oxford Pfeiffer enjoyed specially favourable opportunities for finishing the great edition of Callimachus which he had been planning from the start of his career. Here he found the Oxyrhynchus papyri and their incomparable editor, Edgar Lobel; and here he had the help and company of such distinguished friends and countrymen as Paul Maas and Eduard Fraenkel. The edition of the fragments, with full commentary, appeared in 1949, dedicated to the two Oxford institutions which had sheltered the editor, Campion Hall and Corpus Christi College; the edition of the hymns and epigrams followed four years later. The former volume, in particular, is of exemplary excellence, not surpassed even by Housman's Manilius. But Pfeiffer is far more than a superb technician; his whole work is permeated by a generous and enlightened open-mindedness strongly reminiscent of the humanists to whose study he is devoted.

A series of distinguished articles, beginning early in his career, some

---

* A review of *History of Classical Scholarship from 1300 to 1850* by Rudolf Pfeiffer in *The Times Literary Supplement*, 20 August 1976.

of which are reprinted in the indispensable *Ausgewählte Schriften* of 1959, showed Pfeiffer to have an expert knowledge of the history of classical scholarship, and especially that of the period between the fourteenth and seventeenth centuries; and since the appearance of his Callimachus his major book upon the subject has been awaited perhaps more eagerly than any work of a classical scholar known to be in progress. The need for such a work was very great. Sir John Sandys's history of classical scholarship in three volumes, published in the early years of this century, is a very useful book, but it is little more than a collection of facts and dates.

The sketch of the subject which Wilamowitz published in 1921 (soon to appear in English translation) is written with profound learning and authority, despite certain errors and injustices; but it is only eighty pages long, and something on a larger scale was needed. Pfeiffer's volume dealing with the history of classical scholarship down to the end of the Hellenistic age appeared in 1968, and was received with general admiration. We must rejoice that he has followed the late Eduard Fraenkel's advice to pass by the Middle Ages and go straight to the fourteenth century, thus avoiding an area which might have endlessly detained him – Varro alone might occupy a lifetime – and entering a territory where he moves with unrivalled ease and certainty.

The new volume, *History of Classical Scholarship from 1300 to 1850*, is a wonderful achievement, though because of the author's great age it does not quite satisfy the high expectations with which we have awaited it. It is a short book, but its brevity is among its greatest merits. Pfeiffer has rightly chosen to concentrate on the most important men and topics, and he goes straight for the central issues with the sureness and directness of a great master; his vast knowledge of details never blurs the clarity of the general outline. By means of concise and well-judged footnotes he guides us to the relevant literature as no other scholar could have done, singling out for mention just those details which are most illuminating. The English is not that of an Englishman, but its very foreignness has charm, like the slight foreign accent of a welcome visitor from abroad. It does not matter that a number of small errors and inconsistencies, mostly connected with proper names, have escaped notice. Perhaps consistency in the matter of Renaissance names can hardly be demanded; but Bywater's plea that we should refer to Renaissance scholars, as they did themselves, by their Latin and not their vernacular names ought not to be forgotten. The book is as enjoyable as it is learned and intelligent, and even readers with no claim to classical scholarship will find it as delightful as it is instructive.

One of the most awkward problems that confronts a historian of classical scholarship is that of setting limits to his subject. How much, for instance, should he say about the study of art and archaeology? If these topics are treated in detail, a far longer work, and one requiring specialized knowledge not easily combined with that of literary scholarship, will result; if they are omitted, the treatment even of literary scholarship will be incomplete. The same is true of the study of ancient history, and of the history of education during the period covered. In all these cases Pfeiffer handles the problem with great discretion; he ventures as far into this territory as he needs to, and no further.

But how is the historian of classical scholarship to handle the history and the culture of the period his history covers? Surely he must show how the scholars of each succeeding age have used the study of the ancient world to serve the needs of their own time, and how their picture of that world was conditioned by and itself conditioned the atmosphere of the age in which they lived. Much of the fascination of this book is due to the masterly way in which Pfeiffer has done this; down to the seventeenth century, at least, the interaction of classical studies with contemporary life is presented with a singular unity and fluency. The existence of such an excellent general account, supplying such valuable guidance to specialists in every part of the field covered, will serve as a keen stimulus to future studies. Our chief need now is for detailed studies giving an exact description of the actual procedures of scholars in successive periods of the history of the subject; and here books like E.J. Kenney's history of the classical text, Silvia Rizzo's study of the technical vocabulary of the humanist and Sebastiano Timpanaro's account of the genesis of the so-called 'method of Lachmann' point the way.

The interest of the book is by no means diminished by its being written from a point of view different from that of almost all other histories of its subject. It has been assumed that a historian of classical scholarship must write from a Protestant point of view. Wilamowitz is an obvious instance; and Mark Pattison, almost the only Englishman to have done distinguished work in this field, whose merits Pfeiffer generously acknowledges, saw a direct connection between Roman Catholicism and reactionary obscurantism. The great period of French scholarship ended, Pattison could point out, with Henri IV's acceptance of the mass and the consequent flight of Scaliger to Holland and Casaubon to England. Italy produced no Greek scholar of note between Petrus Victorius in the sixteenth and Leopardi in the nineteenth century; the atmosphere of the Counter-Reformation, Pattison could argue, was not favourable to Greek scholarship. Since the Reformation, far more famous classical scholars have been

Protestant than have been Catholic.

But Pfeiffer's history takes a distinctive colour from his Catholicism, which is very different from the intolerant bigotry of the Counter-Reformation zealots. He warns against the nineteenth-century error of seeing the humanists of the fourteenth and fifteenth centuries as pagans, or as tending towards paganism; rather they were Christians who tried to improve their Christianity by making use of the culture of the ancient world. This attitude informs a wonderful opening section on 'The Renewal of Classical Scholarship in the Italian Renaissance'. Pfeiffer is well aware of the existence of those twelfth-century Paduan humanists whom Giuseppe Billanovich has so brilliantly brought to light. Yet he firmly insists on starting with Petrarch, before whose time he finds no humanism in his sense; Petrarch he can compare with the shadowy Philitas as 'both poet and critic'. He writes superbly about Petrarch and about 'the radiant figure of Politian'.

It is refreshing to find him castigating Georg Voigt, the learned author of the standard nineteenth-century work on the first century of humanism, for having 'called the literary, educational and religious aims of the Italians childish and fantastic, and regretted their lack of Teutonic soul'. Valla, he points out, attacked the Donation of Constantine in order to remove a dangerous misunderstanding, and not in order to attack the papacy; he ended his days as a papal secretary. This is true; and yet certain features of Valla's work, such as his interest in the philosophy of Epicurus, helped to lead the way to developments not easily to be imagined in times when the least suspicion of unorthodoxy might be dangerous. The splendid invective of Valla against the author of the Donation – 'oratio ... alicuius clerici stolidi ... saginati et crassi, ac inter crapulam interque fervorem vini has sententias et haec verba eructantis' – suggests, like other phenomena of the period, a certain impatience with some tendencies of the ecclesiastical establishment.

A powerful chapter on Erasmus, where Pfeiffer builds on without merely repeating his famous article of 1955, forms the core of the second section, entitled 'Humanism and Scholarship in the Netherlands and Germany'. As always, his special sympathy lies with Erasmus, whose *philosophia Christi* aimed to purify religion by an infusion of what was best in the spirit of antiquity, while resisting fanatical intolerance and promoting sound sense and philosophic moderation. Pfeiffer does not cite H.R. Trevor-Roper's demonstration that the chief apostles of reason during the sixteenth and seventeenth centuries were not Calvinists, but Erasmians, but he would certainly accept it. Like Trevor-Roper, he brings out the tragedy of Erasmus' magnificent attempt to avert a breach between the Church and the reformers; but he rightly denies that Erasmus' work was a failure and goes on to trace his influence, first upon those German humanists on whom he has already thrown much light. He notes that in the Netherlands the leading spirits were not Calvinists but Arminians; and he observes the link between Grotius and Erasmus.

Pfeiffer deplores the violence, physical and verbal, of both sides in the French wars of religion, which he sees as 'a national struggle for power'. He brilliantly describes the great scholars of sixteenth-century France, above all Joseph Scaliger. He reminds us that over against the Catholic fanaticism of the early seventeenth century stood a kind of humanistic revival, whose greatest representative was St François de Sales and which led directly to the achievements of the great French Benedictines in palaeography and in patristic studies. He mentions that the Jesuits were active in scholarship during that period, but says little of the restricted nature of their interests, or of the challenge to the authenticity of the charters on which Benedictine foundations depended that occasioned the study of ancient documents by Mabillon and Montfaucon.

There have been two renascences of interest in ancient literature. The first started in the thirteenth century and ended with the religious quarrels of the seventeenth century and with the Battle of the Books, marking the epoch at which France decided that she could manage without the guidance of the ancient classics; the second got under way before the end of the seventeenth century and reached its peak in Germany during the nineteenth and early twentieth. This book teaches us a great deal about the second renascence; but its account of this is by no means as complete and as satisfying as its picture of the first.

The third section 'From the French Renaissance to the German Neohellenism', contains an excellent account of Bentley, showing his importance in the development of new critical methods. Pfeiffer shows that his plan for an edition of the New Testament, never carried out, would have continued the work of Erasmus and anticipated that of Lachmann; Bentley took no notice of the damaging distinction between 'sacred' and 'classical' philology. He assigns a surprising degree of importance to Bentley's Boyle Lectures in defence of Anglican theology against the deists, where he finds 'a characteristic blend of his Christian theology with his humanistic scholarship and his firm grasp of principles'; he finds in three British clergymen, Swift, Berkeley and Bentley, 'the most powerful defenders of the classical, as well as of the Christian tradition, against deists and freethinkers'. Were deists and freethinkers against the classical tradition? A Yorkshire squire who unlike Bentley did not consider the faculties of the human soul as a decisive argument for the existence of a deity wrote that Bentley had 'taken the wrong sow by the ear'; not all readers will disagree with him. Some of Bentley's contemporaries and successors piled up useful stores of information; others did brilliant detailed work; and both helped to prepare for the great age of classical learning that was to follow. But it is impossible not to detect in the scholarship of this period a weakening of the close links with contemporary culture that had existed up to the beginning of the seventeenth century.

These links were reestablished by the scholars of the first period of what Pfeiffer calls 'German Neohellenism', to which the fourth section of his book is devoted. That section starts with a treatment of Winckelmann that is as perceptive as it is learned, and well shows the nature and extent of that great writer's influence; Pfeiffer rightly notes the importance of his awareness of the comprehensive view of the study of the ancient world taken by J.J. Scaliger. He has the finest appreciation of the age of Goethe, as we know from the paper on 'Goethe and the Greek Spirit' which he published as long ago as 1934; yet the great age of German scholarship is far less congenial to him than the age of Petrarch or of Erasmus. Few of its leading figures were Christians, and though now at last Greek literature in its original form and not in Latin dress became widely known to educated Europeans, its influence did not lead men in the direction of the Church. The greatest Hellenists of the time did not regard Greek literature and thought as a mere preparation for the Christian revelation.

This fourth section of the work is written with the same vast learning as the rest. Pfeiffer's brief sketches of Hermann, Welcker, Boeckh and other great figures of the time tell us more in a few pages than others could in volumes; so does his account of Wolf, although in reaction against Wilamowitz he seems to me to rate Heyne too low and Wolf too high. But in this section of the book the relation of classical studies to the general culture of the age is far less clearly indicated than in the earlier sections; this must be partly due to the great complexity of the cultural history of the time, but it is partly due also to the writer's less than perfect sympathy with the age he is describing. We find here rather more than a page about Niebuhr, but only two sentences (the last) about Mommsen, who Pfeiffer says 'did more than anyone else to further the forces of historicism and realism'.[1]

---

[1] See G. Chiarini's review of Pfeiffer's book in *Annali della Scuola Normale Superiore di Pisa*, serie iii, vol. vii, 4 (1977), 1629f., and Silvia Rizzo's in *Rivista di Filologia e di Istruzione Classica* 106 (1978), 354f.; see also my *Blood for the Ghosts*, ch. 22.

Pfeiffer's explanation of the meaning of the term 'humanism' would surprise those who imagine that a humanist means a provincial preacher of dogmatic atheism. The whole book, together with the former volume, constitutes an explanation and exemplification of humanism in its truest sense which, quite apart from the enormous learning it contains, will be of great and lasting value.

3

The Tradition of Erasmus

Professor Pfeiffer's friends and admirers in this country will be heartily grateful to his colleagues in Munich for the way in which they have chosen to celebrate his seventieth birthday. No Festschrift could be so precious as a selection from the writings of one of the greatest scholars of our time. This selection has been made in consultation with the author; and though no choice could content every reader, all will agree that the articles here reprinted give an excellent notion of the man and his work. The book has been admirably edited by Dr Winfried Bühler, who has supplied it with a useful index; and it contains a valuable bibliography of virtually all Pfeiffer's writings.

Pfeiffer is both a great Greek scholar and a great historian of scholarship; and the space available in this book has been evenly divided between these two main activities. The author is known above all for his massive contribution to the understanding of Callimachus, beginning in 1921 with the appearance in H. Lietzmann's *Kleine Texte* of his *editio minor* of the fragments that had become known since Schneider's edition, and culminating in his great Oxford edition of 1949-53. But of the many important articles on Callimachus published during that period, only that on the prologue of the *Aitia* has been reprinted. These pieces are all in some measure superseded by the great book itself, and one can easily sympathise with their author's unwillingness to reprint them; yet they remain essential reading for the scholar seriously interested in this poet, who will study them with due regard to the date of their first appearance. Not unnaturally the volume contains the four important pieces dealing with Hellenistic poetry published in English during Pfeiffer's residence in this country (1938-51), which are less accessible in Germany than his other writings. Otherwise, the first half of the book is entirely devoted to articles on early epic and on tragedy; except that it contains the polished lecture entitled 'Gottheit und Individuum in

* A review of *Ausgewählte Schriften: Aufsätze und Vorträge zur griechischen Dichtung und zum Humanismus* by Rudolf Pfeiffer in *Classical Review* 11 (1961), 125f.

der frühgriechischen Lyrik' with which Pfeiffer inaugurated his tenure of the chair at Freiburg in 1928. The papers in the second come, for the most part, from less accessible periodicals, and will be less familiar to the public. Written with profound learning, and in a style that combines clarity, elegance, and charm, they range over the whole history of scholarship from the Renaissance to the present day; yet the view of scholarship, and indeed of life, that emerges from them has a singular consistency. Pfeiffer has always shown a special interest in Erasmus; and this book contains a brilliant sketch of his career, setting right the popular misconceptions that make him out an eighteenth-century rationalist before his time, advocating a semi-pagan religion of aesthetics that retained Christian ethics while jettisoning Christian dogma. Pfeiffer shows how Erasmus rightly regarded himself as a follower of Clement, Origen, and Augustine in the attempt to bring about a union between Christianity and the humanism of the ancient world, and how his critical scholarship, far from cultivating aestheticism or erudition for its own sake, never ceased to be systematically directed to that end. In order to prove that Erasmian humanism can be blended with Christian religion, even in the person of a saint, Pfeiffer movingly appeals to the example of Thomas More, *omnium horarum homo*.

Pfeiffer's interest in Erasmus gives the key to his whole conception of scholarship; for it is impossible to read this book without seeing that the author himself is a confirmed believer in the *philosophia Christi* that Erasmus conceived. Erasmus pleaded for what he called *libertas spiritus* in the name of religion itself; for the critical study that was urgently necessary in order to free the texts of the Bible and the Fathers from corruptions and accretions could do only good to the cause of religious truth. A sketch of the Benedictine contribution to learning and education acknowledges the author's debt to the Benedictine foundation of St Stephan where he received his early education; and he concludes his account of Wilhelm von Humboldt, the scholar and philologist, diplomat and administrator, who played so great a part in laying the foundations of the great resurgence of German culture that followed the defeat of Napoleon, by an expression of regret that religion was absent from Humboldt's noble and idealistic view of life. In fact singularly few great classical scholars have been devout Catholics; but Pfeiffer's belief never narrows his sympathies or affects his severe critical standards. He shows, for example, profound sympathy with Goethe and with Wilamowitz, neither of whom possessed an *anima naturaliter Christiana*.

The essay concerned with Goethe aims at vindicating him against Nietzsche's charge that he did not truly understand the ancient

Greeks. Pfeiffer shows, with great lucidity and penetration, that Goethe's view of the universe and of man's place in it is much indebted to and in some ways closely resembles that of the Greeks before Plato. Yet he does not go closely into the details of Nietzsche's criticism; and the reader may well be left with the impression that, despite the genuine Hellenism that was an important factor in his thought, Goethe stood too close to the classicism of Winckelmann and his generation to appreciate to the full the powerful elements which Nietzsche called 'Dionysiac' and which scholars since his time have done so much to illuminate.

Perhaps the most delightful essay in the book is that upon Conrad Peutinger, the town chronicler of Pfeiffer's native city of Augsburg during the first part of the sixteenth century, who played an important part at the Diet of Worms and did pioneer work in the study of Roman remains in Germany. Peutinger was a man of affairs who enjoyed the confidence of the Emperor Maximilian and a scholar of international importance who had links with Erasmus and his English disciples and with Politian and the Florentine circle of Ficino. But Pfeiffer shows how firmly he was rooted in his own city of Augsburg, one of those ancient civic communities whose intellectual life, like that of the Nuremberg of Dürer and Pirckheimer, reached far back into the Middle Ages. He quotes the charming letters, written in excellent Latin, which Peutinger's daughter sent him during his long absences; he describes the *sodalitas literaria Augustana*, including among its members distinguished citizens of many different professions; and he shows the importance to Peutinger of his close connection with the neighbouring Benedictine Abbey of St Ulrich. Reading this essay, it is impossible not to see how much of this humane and civilised tradition in South Germany has survived, in spite of everything, into the present time, and that this writer's interest in his subject is no mere pious antiquarianism.

The photograph of Professor Pfeiffer that serves as frontispiece is an excellent likeness; and the book itself gives a true portrait of a scholar whose writings deserve the close attention of any reader who cares for Greek scholarship and for humane studies.

.4

Classical Influences on European Culture
1500-1700

Whatever one may feel about the publication of the acts of learned conferences, the 1500-1700 volume of *Classical Influences on European Culture*, like its predecessor relating to the period 500-1500, contains some excellent contributions, which together with full bibliographies and admirable indexes make a valuable book. In the past many scholars dealing with this subject have had a purely classical training, and have tended to value humanistic literature only for the classical elements that it preserves. For many years now it has been generally recognised that this is unrewarding; it is infinitely more interesting to see how the Renaissance writer or artist has seen the classical material at his disposal, and how he has combined it with other elements to create a new product suited to his own requirements. A good knowledge of the classics is necessary for the effective pursuit of Renaissance studies; but the classical scholar who engages in them must know and understand as much of the Renaissance atmosphere as he can, just as the Renaissance scholar will find it helpful to learn all he can of the classics and the mode of their transmission. The greatest living authority in this field, Rudolf Pfeiffer (astonishingly, not mentioned in this book) is a classical scholar of great eminence; but he values the age of the humanists for its own sake, and is intimately acquainted with its history and its culture.

What emerges clearly from these essays, as from all the best modern work on this subject, is that the use made of the classics by the humanists of this age was above all else practical. Few of these men were in any significant degree pagans or aesthetes; most of them were Christians, and most of them used ancient literature and art to act upon the modern world. This is most evident in the case of the many who studied ancient works for their scientific or technological content.

* A review of *Classical Influences on European Culture: 1550-1700* edited by R.R. Bolgar in *The Times Literary Supplement*, 25 June 1976.

Medicine, mathematics and astronomy, law and government, art and architecture are familiar instances; all the same, one is surprised to learn from the informative paper of G. Oestreich that between 1490 and 1597/8 there appeared no less than 660 editions of Galen, eighteen of them containing his voluminous complete works. Most of these were translations, needed by doctors simply because better medical textbooks were not then available. Less widely known is the regular use of ancient works on agriculture, mining, military science and various branches of technology. The elder Pliny, whose vast encyclopedia in thirty-seven books appeared in forty-six editions before 1550, was valued for his content rather than his style.

Since the humanists of this age were practical, they needed also to be independent. C. Vasoli shows how they advanced from criticising their contemporaries for their inferiority to the ancients to criticising the ancients themselves, sometimes by the ancients' own standards but sometimes by those of the new culture which they themselves with the aid of the ancients had created. J.C. Margolin shows how Vives both used and criticised Plato and Aristotle in a spirit far removed from that of medieval Platonism or Aristotelianism. H. Weber shows how Bodin made skilful use of Aristotle's *Ethics* and *Politics* in constructing a new and independent political theory designed to justify the absolute monarchy of his own nation. H. Dörrie shows how Lucan came to be criticised (in the age of the baroque!) in the name of those ancient theorists who held that poetry should be simple, truthful and conformable to nature. N. Dacos demonstrates the independent use made of Nero's Golden House by Raphael in the designing of his Logge; and T. Buddensieg, continuing the reflections on the impact made upon succeeding ages by the Pantheon begun in the proceedings of the earlier conference, gives further evidence for the mixture of respect and independence shown by Renaissance architects in their dealings with the ancient masters.

No new idea put forward in the volume is more intriguing than Sir Anthony Blunt's suggestion that Borromini derived his inspiration for the lantern of St Ivo and the *trompe l'oeil* colonnade in the Palazzo Spada from the drawings of the Milanese architect Montanus (1534-1621), purporting to show reconstructions of ancient works, which are in Sir John Soane's Museum. Sir Anthony justifies Borromini's plea that he was not, as his enemies claimed, a destroyer of classical principles, but their upholder.

The practicality of the humanists is nowhere more evident than in the sphere of religion. Most humanists were Christians, and many used their humanism to purify and to intensify their Christianity. From their different points of view Pfeiffer and H.R. Trevor-Roper have both argued that Erasmus was above all else a Christian writer, setting far greater store on his work on the Bible and the Fathers than on his study of the classics, and hoping to reinspire the Church by means of a *philosophia Christi* based on the renewed investigation of its own early history. E.F. Rice and A.H.T. Levi provide evidence for this view, and J.B. Trapp seconds it by drawing attention to the great quantity of biblical exegesis written, though left unpublished, by Erasmus' close friend John Colet. Professor Levi is right in saying that there is something in common between the purposes of Erasmus and those of Ignatius de Loyola; Calvin too started his career as an Erasmian humanist; yet how great a difference in temper separates the great humanist from the fanatics of the Counter-Reformation period on both sides!

This volume contains very little about anti-Christian elements in the culture of the period; but it contains a remarkable paper by R.H. Popkin, the historian of scepticism, about the movement called Preadamism. Even during the Middle Ages the doctrine that all men were descended from Adam had given rise to doubts, and the discovery of America lent these doubts new substance. During the seventeenth century Isaac La Peyrère, a Frenchman descended from converted Jews, combined with a curious French nationalist Messianism a theory of human origins which made some pertinent criticisms of received doctrines. La Peyrère was silenced by religious orthodoxy, but Spinoza, Bayle and Voltaire did not fail to note his arguments.

The Latin literature of this period, hardly less than the vernacular literature, at its best shows an independence which lifts it high above the level of slavish imitation. Such work does not deserve the neglect and contempt which has resulted from the excessive concentration on the classics shown by Renaissance scholars in the past. This injustice is now beginning to be remedied, though as several contributors point out the lack of adequate texts, catalogues and other aids is a severe handicap. John Sparrow sets out the plan of the anthology of neo-Latin verse which he is preparing in collaboration with Alessandro Perosa[1] in the hope of doing for the Latin poetry of this period what F.J.E. Raby did for the Latin poetry of the Middle Ages.

Few have done more to show what opportunities some of this poetry offers to a scholar properly equipped to study it than Walther Ludwig in his editions of the *Stephanium* of Joannes Harmonius Marsus and the *Michaelida* of Ziliolus of Ferrara; and Professor Ludwig contributes to

---

[1] Alessandro Perosa and John Sparrow (eds), *Renaissance Latin Verse: an Anthology* (1979); see below, ch. 5.

this book a most attractive study of the sixteenth-century German poet Petrus Lotichius Secundus, whose beautiful elegy describing how he returned to his home near Heidelberg to find the country devastated by war is a fine specimen of the kind of work the new anthology will make available. J. IJsewijn sketches the history of neo-Latin satire, a field in which everything remains to be done.

The humanists of this period were much preoccupied with style, but even in this preoccupation their practicality is apparent. Men like Erasmus and Valla cared about style not merely for aesthetic reasons, but because they wished to improve the clarity of thinking together with the clarity of writing, and to eliminate the muddled argument together with the prolix verbiage of the later Middle Ages. The Ciceronianism of the early Italians had come to a point where it was substituting one kind of empty verbosity for another; it had, therefore, to be got out of the way. Lisa Jardine stresses the importance of Valla's exposition of dialectic, by which he meant a kind of argumentation based on the enthymeme as well as the syllogism and better suited to the needs of literature and life than the barren pedantries of scholastic formal logic.

Rudolph Agricola developed the subject further, and Gabriel Harvey made it the basis of his Cambridge teaching. Quintilian was an important author in this connection. In a general way W.S. Howell is right to reiterate his argument of twenty years ago that rhetoric, logic and poetics were in this age distinct and developed each its own separate literature; although in practice they shade into one another too often for this formula in its simplest form to be quite adequate.

Very typical of our own time is the devotion of a large amount of space to the collections of common-places which were so widely used during the period the volume covers. Ravisius Textor's vast collection of epithets, first published in 1518 and regularly reprinted until 1664, is dealt with in two articles, an elegant and succinct one by I.D. McFarlane and an informative but ponderous one by Walter J. Ong. The common-places belong to a tradition which goes back to antiquity; Fr Ong somewhat underestimates the prevalence of florilegia and gnomologies at that time, as a glance at Henry Chadwick's introduction to his edition of the *Sentences of Sextus*, or at J.W.B. Barns's account of ancient gnomologies will show.[2]

Their ultimate origins may well be found in oral culture; but the period we are concerned with is highly literary, and the curious framework derived from that modern master Marshall McLuhan with which Fr Ong surrounds this treatment of the topic seems to me not

[2] *CQ* 44 (1950), 126f. and n.s. 1 (1951) 1f.

particularly helpful. But it is useful to the scholar to be able to recognise the commonplaces, as M.A. Screech and D. Coleman both remind us. For instance, Du Bellay in Sonnet 140 writes:

> Aymes donques (Ronsard) comme pouvant haïr;
> Haïs donques (Ronsard) comme pouvant aymer.

Professor Screech thinks Du Bellay took the sentiment from the Roman mime-writer Publilius Syrus, who wrote: 'ita amicum habeas ut facile fieri hunc inimicum putes.' But Du Bellay studied Sophocles in the original with the best teachers, and the words of Ajax at 1.678f. of Sophocles's play named after him are very close to his: 'I am newly aware that one must hate an enemy as one who in time may be a friend, and that I shall be willing to help a friend only while remembering that he may not be a friend for ever.' It is worth knowing that Du Bellay probably took the notion from a far greater author than Publilius Syrus.

In general there is far less in the book about Greek, except for Plato and Aristotle and the Greek fathers, than there is about Latin. That is partly due to the nature of the facts. Until the middle of the eighteenth century, most Europeans saw the Greeks through Roman spectacles; not before then was there a reasonably large public able to read Greek in the original.

But sixteenth-century France made a tremendous advance in Greek studies; its humanists, knowing that they could hardly hope to rival the Italians in Latin, set out to master Greek, which despite the achievements of the isolated genius Politian remained largely an uncharted field. This book says little about Turnebus, Auratus and Lambinus and the relations of the poets of the Pléiade with the scholars of their time; it says little about J.J. Scaliger and Casaubon, who Dr Bolgar seems to imagine were important chiefly for what they did for textual criticism. Apart from his virtual discovery of the earliest Latin writers and all his other purely classical achievements, the younger Scaliger combined with classical learning a knowledge of oriental languages and of science and mathematics that enabled him to make a contribution to historical studies whose importance extends far beyond the confines of ancient history. But the volume would have done better justice to sixteenth-century France if Carlotta Griffiths could have been persuaded to let it contain her study of Janus Parrhasius, whose devotion to Greek led him to espouse the ugly daughter of Demetrius Chalcondyles and whose commentary on Claudian's poem on the rape of Proserpine displays much Greek learning.

In his introduction to the earlier collection Dr Bolgar writes that the achievements in textual criticism of Bentley, Lachmann and Wilamowitz 'belong to an age when classical writings had ceased to make a really important direct contribution to man's intellectual growth'. Does he think that Greek literature and philosophy made no important contribution to intellectual growth in the age of Goethe? or in that of Nietzsche? or in our own time?

5

Renaissance Latin Verse

Victorian romanticism looked down its nose upon the Latin poetry of the Renaissance; how could verse not written in the vernacular language of the poets display the 'freshness' and 'sincerity' which it demanded? The prejudice has died hard; the pompous cliché that all such poetry must be 'stillborn' was uttered by an author so recently deceased as C.S. Lewis. But this verse is not only important for any serious student of the culture of its time, as Burckhardt demonstrated in a dozen brilliant pages of his book on the subject: much of it has great literary merit. Anyone who doubts it should read the splendid essay on 'Latin Verse of the High Renaissance' which Mr Sparrow contributed to the *Italian Renaissance Studies* dedicated to the memory of Cecilia Ady and edited by Ernest Jacob which appeared 15 years ago. But till now the reader persuaded by that argument has had no standard anthology to turn to as the student of medieval Latin poetry may turn to the Oxford Book of Latin Verse and the other collections made by F.J.E. Raby.

This gap has now been filled in the most satisfactory way by two editors particularly well qualified for the task. Professor Perosa has been known as one of the leading authorities in the field at least since his publication in 1951 of an admirable edition of the poems of one of the most distinguished poets and scholars of the period, Michael Marullus. As for Mr Sparrow, his exceptional gifts as a scholar would have found more recognition if he had made distinguished contributions to fewer branches of learning and if he had less taste and eloquence and less obvious enthusiasm for literature. In this book the talents of both editors are seen to great advantage. The brief accounts of each author and the notes give the reader much help with small space. The necessary bibliographical information is given, and yet the learning of the editors never swamps the reader. To reproduce the spelling of the manuscripts would have caused inconsistency as well as

* A review of *Renaissance Latin Verse* edited by Alessandro Perosa and John Sparrow in the *Spectator*, 24 February 1979.

obscurity, and the editors have sensibly modernised throughout. The text has been most carefully edited, and the book contains some felicitous emendations; for an example see p. 499, where no previous editor has seen that the English antiquary Leland was latinising the Greek word for 'squirrel'. But the book is not only a distinguished work of scholarship; it contains much poetry that is a delight to read, and its superb printing and production and the low price at which the generosity of All Souls College has allowed it to be offered make it a most valuable possession.

The principles adopted by the editors in choosing poems have been set out by Mr Sparrow in *Classical Influences on European Culture: 1500-1700* (ed. R. Bolgar, 1976). Petrarch and Boccaccio are the only fourteenth-century authors included; all the rest belong to the fifteenth and sixteenth centuries. Very rightly, 319 out of the 560 pages are devoted to Italian poets; of the remainder, 58 pages go to the French and 57 to the Germans. Extracts of long poems are included, so that there are specimens of didactic poetry and of secular and religious epic. Thus we find here passages from Petrarch's epic poem *Africa*, whose hero is Scipio Africanus, and which he valued far more than any of his verses in Italian; and we have passages from Sannazaro's once immensely popular poem on the birth of Christ, *De Partu Virginis*, which whatever one may feel about its strange mingling of Christian and pagan mythology is a far better work than the once equally successful religious epics of Mantuan and Vida. Marullus, a gloomy and quarrelsome refugee from Constantinople, was not only a fine scholar but a true poet; he made a distinguished contribution to the textual criticism of Lucretius (see Munro's introduction) and in his *Hymni Naturales* he strikes a genuinely Lucretian note. We have also a sample of the poem which the distinguished doctor Fracastoro names after the nymph Syphilis, whose name has ever since been borne by the disease for which she is responsible. Marcellus Palingenius in the *Zodiacus Vitae* performs the difficult feat of addressing the Supreme Being at considerable length without doing anything to distress the reader.

But the greater part of the book's contents consists of various kinds of occasional poetry. Politian's elegy on the death of Albiera degli Albizzi challenges and stands up to comparison with the great elegy of Propertius on Cornelia. No poem in the book is more moving than the same writer's lament for Lorenzo il Magnifico; despite the scepticism of the learned editors, I am attracted by the suggestion of the Florentine jurist Ugo Enrico Paoli that the metrical elements of this are taken from Greek lyric, and put together in a fashion suggested by the lyrics in the tragedies of Seneca. The occasional verses of Pontanus fully justify his great reputation among his contemporaries, particularly the lullabies he wrote for his children and his lament for his son Lucio. By way of contrast Vida's threnody for his parents seems to me overdone. Marullus impresses as greatly in his short as in his longer poems. He is one of the few poets in the collection who make effective use of metres taken from Horatian lyric; as Burckhardt observed, in general Catullus proved a safer model. Niccolò d'Arco's lament for his mother, who died while he was a child, has reminded Mr Sparrow of Cowper's verses on a similar occasion. Hardly less moving are the dying address to his friends of the gay and dissipated Francesco Molza and the lament of the French poet Jean Macrin for his 'coniunx blanda et amabilis'.

Mr Sparrow finds that the love-poetry of these poets has been over-praised: 'when they write about love,' he says, 'these poets tend to become shallow, imitative, monotonous.' Their amatory verse improves, he thinks, only when it becomes less pleasant, as when Niccolò d'Arco addressing a male person reminds one of the bitterest strain in Horace ('nonne vides uti/virus nescio quod meo/dirum continuo stillet ab inguin?'), or when the 'harsh, ingenious, difficult, ugly, coarse' poet Lancino Corti, who has reminded him of Donne, complains that he has reached a stage at which the need to make love is on a level with other natural appetites. Among the poets who wrote love-poems in their youth several became Cardinals, one Pope, and one, even more surprisingly, Calvin's successor at Geneva. Ovid's *Heroides* inspired some interesting poems; Molza put into the mouth of Catherine of Aragon a dignified remonstrance against Henry VIII, and Basinio Basini, one of the humanists at the court of Rimini, wrote two moving letters supposed to pass between the ruthless but cultivated despot Sigismondo Malatesta and his beautiful and adored wife Isotta degli Atti.

Many poems in the book are written by men better known for other activities. Erasmus as a poet is interesting, but comes nowhere near Erasmus as a prose writer. More, on the other hand, contributes touching verses written to a never-forgotten childhood love and an affectionate epistle to his children; we also find him in fierce controversy with the French humanist Germain de Brie. Boccaccio and Pico della Mirandola are each represented by a single very creditable specimen. Filelfo's verse is interesting, but not particularly distinguished; Ariosto's Latin poetry is admirable, especially his epitaphs for Raphael and himself; Castiglione's contributions increase one's admiration for the author of *Il Cortegiano*. The great Chancellor of France, Michel de l'Hôpital, who tried courageously to save his country from the disaster of the wars of religion, is the author of splendid epistles in the Horatian manner. Du Bellay is admirable in Latin; his epitaph on a dog runs, 'Latratu fures excepi, mutus amantes; sic placui domino, sic placui dominae.' Ulrich von Hutten and Melanchthon were competent versifiers, though hardly in the class of their compatriot, the Heidelberg doctor Lotichius, who died at thirty-two. Seen in this company, the Dutchman Johannes Secundus and the Scotchman George Buchanan hardly live up to the claims made for them by their countrymen.

6

Americans and German Scholarship
1770-1870

When the modest colleges of America were transformed into great modern universities, the model was supplied by Germany; very naturally, for during the nineteenth century when this occurred, the German universities were by far the best in Europe. At this time many Americans went to study in Germany; the number seems to have been between nine and ten thousand.

Until lately Americans looked on these facts with satisfaction; a somewhat rosy view was taken as to how much the American visitors learnt from their German hosts. But now that revolt against the tyranny of the doctoral dissertation and the demand that it shall make 'an original contribution to knowledge' is spreading widely, a different attitude is beginning to be expressed. Carl Diehl, whose own book originated in a Yale dissertation, is by no means wholly convinced that the American love affair with German scholarship was a good thing.

Readers who wish to learn just what German scholarship during its greatest period was like would be unwise to rely wholly on Dr Diehl. He has heard that it finally petered out into something called historicism, which as Nietzsche pointed out led to dryness, excessive technicality, and the piling up of learned matter for its own sake. He knows that classical philology had at this time a special importance even for the methods of other humanistic disciplines, and therefore concentrates upon it. In theory he starts at 1770, because the great movement in scholarship got under way as early as this; but he gives a central place to F.A. Wolf and to the famous book in which he began the modern discussion of the Homeric question. Wolf, as one of the creators of the new philology and as Wilhelm von Humboldt's chief academic collaborator in the foundation of the University of Berlin, is

* A review of *Americans and German Scholarship 1770-1870* by Carl Diehl in *The Times Literary Supplement*, 23 June 1978.

indeed a representative figure. But it may be doubted whether his book on Homer is the work best calculated to exemplify the characteristics of the new scholarship, even if its importance is correctly estimated. Dr Diehl seems to think that its main significance lay in its denial to anyone except professional scholars 'the right to read, let alone criticise or enjoy Homer'. In fact the essential content of Wolf's theory depended upon attitudes and assumptions that were widespread in his time, which helps to show why it aroused so much interest outside academic circles. Wolf's theory appealed to those who had admired Ossian.

The most interesting information Dr Diehl has to give us comes from the correspondence of scholars who studied in Germany from the year 1815, when Edward Everett and George Ticknor left Boston for Göttingen. He divides his period into two sections, the divide coming about 1850. During the first of these, he thinks, the Americans were aware of the inspiration behind German scholarship, but for national and cultural reasons were unable to profit from it; during the second they learnt scholarly technique from their hosts, but became conscious that the inspiration had departed. It is a pity that he stops at the beginning of the Franco-Prussian War, the moment when German culture in general, vulgarised and dehumanised by the materialism of the Bismarckian epoch, was at its nadir. Between then and 1914, a notable cultural revival took place.

Dr Diehl notes a number of despairing or disapproving comments upon Germany made by the visiting Americans; and he rightly observes that nothing like the German scholarship of the great period arose in the United States. He does well to correct the complacency of some former treatments of the subject; yet he has ended by underrating the significance of what the Americans did learn. It is a pity he has concentrated so much on classical studies, which were indeed important for the Germans, but less important for the Americans. It was above all in historical studies that the German influence was to prove important. Indeed German scholarship was not reproduced in America, and not surprisingly, little academic work that was the equal of the best European work was done at first. But the work that was done had great merits as well as great deficiencies; it was modified by German influence, but it was naturally and rightly American; and it led finally to great achievements.

The most important visitor of Dr Diehl's first period was George Bancroft, who (although in Germany he studied classics) was to become the leading American historian of his time. The significance of his German experience is best understood if, in addition to the comments which he wrote home at the time, we consider his career as a whole. Bancroft continued into old age the amazing industry acquired during his German period; and though his historical technique was not surprisingly not that of the later part of the century, he became a very learned man. Naturally his historical standpoint is that of his age and nation. The Puritan ethic was strong in him and he never lost his faith in democracy or in progress, even though his democracy was no longer that of the Adamses but that of Jackson, and his progress not that of the Enlightenment but a God-ordained historical necessity. Unlike the great German but like the chief Roman historians, Bancroft was not only a scholar but a successful diplomatist and statesman. He did not need the inspiration that lay behind German scholarship, because he derived his inspiration from his native culture. But he would hardly have written as he did without the example of the German achievement.

In the second section of his period Dr Diehl mentions several Americans who studied in Germany and came back to have distinguished careers in scholarship. William Dwight Whitney the eminent comparative philologist, James Russell Lowell the literary scholar and critic, and Francis Child the authority on ballads, to take only three, counted for a good deal, and the effect they had on others was more important than their own achievements. The representative figure of American classical scholarship of this time is Basil Lanneau Gildersleeve. Born in Charleston, South Carolina in 1831, he studied at Berlin, Göttingen and Bonn from 1850 to 1853, was wounded in the Civil War, left the University of Virginia for the Johns Hopkins of Daniel Coit Gilman, founded the *American Journal of Philology*, wrote books which are still valuable and lived till 1924.

The belief that Americans studying in Germany got no stimulus from their teachers will not survive an acquaintance with Gildersleeve's writings, a representative sample of which will be found in the selection from his famous column in the *AJP*, 'Brief Mention', which appeared in 1930. In his earlier years he spoke with contempt of English classical scholarship, with its exaggerated emphasis on translation from English into classical languages and its lack of intellectual curiosity. Later in life he modified his strictures and was ready to allow that Americans should be eclectic as they worked towards the creation of a national style. But he stuck to his initial judgment that German work showed 'far more thoroughness and daring and power of research' than English, and he was right.

Classical studies of the Victorian English kind might have given the Americans an extra surface polish; they might have benefited from the tutorial system, as Harvard and Yale benefited from the building of colleges by Harkness much later. But Gildersleeve was right; the sterner discipline of German scholarship was better calculated to correct the deficiencies from which they suffered. The work of those American academics who did imitate the Oxford of Jowett makes one glad that there were not more of them. Dr Diehl shows that President Kirkland had his doubts about German scholarship, in which he was not alone. In spite of this, American scholars produced much valuable work, and laid the foundations of the impressive developments of the following century. Part of the credit for this belongs to the German connection, whatever may be felt about the present condition of the graduate schools.

Dr Diehl does well to point out that the Americans were hindered from taking full advantage of their German training by the weakness of their secondary education, and by the dispute over the extent to which their universities and colleges should take on elementary teaching. Bancroft was quick to realise this; had the modern school which he and his companion in studies in Germany, Joseph Cogswell, established at Round Point, near Northampton, Mass., survived, it might have had an importance out of all proportion to the number of its pupils. In our time America has what are in most respects the greatest universities in the world; the faults of American education lie now, as always, principally in the schools. The sentimentality which forms part of the legacy of Rousseau still prevents children from being made to work seriously at the age when the memory is best; powerful educational societies, consisting largely of fond mothers, have a pernicious influence, as the eminent educationist Arthur C. Bestor has shown us.

In particular, the teaching of languages is deficient. To learn to speak a foreign language well, you need to start early; you need a native teacher, or at least a gramophone; and you need to be obliged to work. Rousseauising softness is not the only factor working against this in the United States. The need to make Americans out of the great mass of immigrants entering the melting-pot has caused speakers of a foreign language to be despised as culturally backward. A Yale professor of Italian origin told me how he shocked his brother, a businessman, by leaving his small daughter in the charge of their old mother, who spoke very little English. 'If you go on like that,' he said, 'she'll grow up speaking Italian!' and was horrified to learn that that was what his brother wanted. The weakness in the schools, where learning often takes second place to processes supposed to promote 'social adjustment', such as the three Ds (Dancing, Debating and Dating) of the headmistress in *Lolita*, obliges students at the university to work extremely hard. It is far harder for an American than for a European to attain real command of Greek or Latin; even nowadays, when America's contribution to classical scholarship is very large, the handicap persists. Thanks to the blessings of 'progressive' education, Europeans may soon be on the same level with Americans in this respect.

The trend in American education that is responsible for the weakness of the schools has far worse effects than that of making life difficult for scholars. American culture derived, from its links with the Enlightenment, no less than from its Protestant religion, a strong universalising tendency. German thinkers, under the influence of Herder, had asserted the autonomy of different cultures and different nations against the universalising rationalism which they associated with French cultural imperialism. While Americans were asserting their autonomy against England, this German attitude might seem congenial; but in the long run it was different from their own, which may help to account for the discontents of American students in nineteenth-century Germany. The trend of which I have spoken is rooted in the generalising simplifications of the Enlightenment and in the dogmatic certainties of evangelical religion. It is fatally combined with a strain of crudely philistine positivism and utilitarianism natural in a people whose culture derives much from English nonconformity, particularly when such a people has had many practical difficulties to struggle with.

Here lies the cause of the assumption that all foreigners would be Americans if they could, the total inability to enter in imagination into alien habits of thought, that remain to this day dangerously common in the United States. In fiction, one thinks of the illusions of Graham Greene's Quiet American; in history, of the handling of foreign affairs by Woodrow Wilson and Franklin Roosevelt. These were expensively educated men; it is in one way comforting, but in another saddening, to remember how much better Harry Truman did. Even if it does not matter very much that no person strongly affected by this isolationist tendency can be wholly civilised, it does matter that no such person can be trusted with the management of international relations.

7

'What is a Classic?'

Professor Kermode has taken as the starting point of his T.S. Eliot Lectures the address 'What is a Classic?' which Eliot delivered as President of the Virgilian Society in 1944. In that lecture Eliot claimed that 'our classic, the classic of all Europe, is Virgil'. He did not mean by this that Virgil was the greatest European poet; he meant that his work showed maturity of mind, maturity of manners, maturity of language and perfection of the common style to such a degree that it provided us with a criterion by which to judge our living poets.

Eliot devoted twenty-seven pages of his lecture to an argument designed to show that Virgil possessed these qualities. Only in the last five pages does he touch upon the special relation to the Roman Empire and to its spiritual continuation throughout European history enjoyed by Virgil in consequence of the subject matter of the *Aereid*. But Professor Kermode seems to assume that Virgil's importance for Eliot lay mainly in his significance as the propagator of an 'imperialist myth' of Latin and Christian cultural continuity.

In his first lecture he gives a learned account of Virgil's influence during the middle ages, with special reference to the imperial myth as it appeared to Dante and to others. In his second, he shows how English poets of the seventeenth century still felt the influence, but rejected the myth; he discusses Marvell and Milton, coming close to agreeing with Christopher Hill that the latter had much in common with the Muggletonians. The eighteenth century, he argues, replaced classicism with Augustanism and had no use for the imperial myth. Addison, in his *Discourse of Ancient and Modern Learning*, recommends the reading of Virgil, but thinks we should try to read him as his contemporaries might have done; his age did not conceive of the poet as prophet, and did not concern itself with the Christian universalist myth of Virgil. Henceforth, Professor Kermode thinks, Virgil was handed over to the philologists as an antiquity.

'The doctrine of classic as model or criterion,' he writes on page

* A review of *The Classic* by Frank Kermode in the *Spectator*, 20 September 1975.

fifteen (but it is really page one; the pagination of this book reminds one of wine-bottles with false bottoms), 'entails, in some form, the assumption that the ancient can be more or less immediately relevant and available, in a sense contemporaneous with modern, or anyway that its nature is such that it can, by strategies of accommodation, be made so. When this assumption is rejected, the whole authority of the classic as model is being challenged, and then we have ... the recurrent *querelle* between the ancient and modern.' Eliot certainly said that Virgil should serve as a critical criterion by which our own poetry could be judged. But nowhere in his essay do I find the word 'model', used twice in the paragraph I have quoted in such a way as to imply that Eliot used it. Many English poets of the eighteenth and even the nineteenth century used Virgil as a model; it might be argued that Wordsworth and Tennyson were among them. But the only poem of Eliot's time modelled on Virgil that I can think of is V. Sackville-West's poem *The Land*; in an age that disliked a grand style and distrusted rhetoric, the idea of Virgil as a model would have been unthinkable. A criterion is by no means the same thing; and Virgil's importance as a criterion has, in Eliot's lecture, very little to do with Virgil as the propagator of an imperial myth.

Professor Kermode now sets out to show how certain modern authors have achieved classic quality by methods different from those of the ancients. The early Americans, he argues in his third lecture, rejected the imperial myth and chose in the early nineteenth century a new past which was not classical but Hebraic; there is truth in this, only we must remember that they did not reject the myth of *republican* Rome, which was alive among them long after the epoch of the founding fathers of their own republic. The first modern author he chooses as an illustration is Hawthorne, stressing in an acute passage that writer's eagerness to leave open more than one interpretation of his characters and their behaviour. 'The classic of the modern imperium,' he writes, gliding from the imperial theme to that of multiplicity of meanings, 'cannot be, as the Bible had been and Virgil too, a repository of certain, unchanging truths.' Whether Hawthorne is a classic in the sense in which that word was used by Eliot he does not enquire; it might be argued that the characteristics of Hawthorne to which Professor Kermode draws attention disqualify him in that respect. Yet it might with better reason be contended that to be a repository of certain unchanging truths is no function of the classic; Eliot certainly never claimed that it was such.

In the fourth lecture Professor Kermode examines *Wuthering Heights*, certainly a work of genius, but perhaps not one which Eliot would have called a classic. Q.D. Leavis in a penetrating essay has ascribed the inconsistencies, which a close examination of the text seems to her and to Professor Kermode to reveal, to the author's failure to eliminate the traces of different earlier versions of the novel which had different artistic aims. Professor Kermode prefers to explain the book's 'recalcitrant elements' as being due to the coexistence of a plurality of significance. Did Emily Brontë mean them all? Professor Kermode's view 'supposes that the reader's share in the novel is not so much a matter of knowing, by heroic efforts of intelligence and divination, what Emily Brontë really meant – and knowing it ... better than she did – as of responding creatively to indeterminacies of meaning inherent in the text and possibly enlarged by the action of time'. (Professor Kermode makes it quite explicit that this last phrase means that the passage of time between the writing of the book and its reading by the modern reader may have changed the situation.) He ends by pleading with us to recognise that 'multiplicity of reading may result from a work's *constructive ambiguity*', this last being an expression borrowed from the linguist Roman Jakobson by the fashionable French critic Roland Barthes, who has made of Racine's dramas, Professor Kermode tells us, 'something unashamedly sexual'. 'If, finally,' he writes, 'we compare this sketch of a modern version of the classic with the imperial classic that occupied me earlier, we see on the one hand that the modern view is necessarily tolerant of change and plurality whereas the older, regarding most forms of plurality as heretical, holds fast to the time-transcending idea of Empire.'

First of all, the 'imperial myth' has nothing whatever to do with the question of whether the reader should allow for 'constructive ambiguities' and other agents of multiplicity of meaning in his author's text; it seems to have been dragged in simply to discredit in the eyes of the speaker's audience the old-fashioned view that a literary text means one thing and one only, which is what the author intended it to mean. It would be most unwise to assert that view in an unqualified form; even E.B. Hirsch, whom Professor Kermode cites as its main proponent in modern times, states it only with qualifying clauses. A work of literary art is not commonly designed, as Professor Kermode seems to imagine Virgil's work to have been, as 'a repository of certain, unchanging truths'; far more often it presents a conflict between different forces or ideas about which different readers will feel differently according to their point of view, and between which even the author may be torn or give the appearance of being torn.

Virgil himself will furnish an example. According to orthodox Roman belief, Aeneas was right to leave Dido, and Virgil knows it; anyone who doubts it should consult an admirable lecture lately published by Mr John Sparrow. But Aeneas did so at great cost to his

personal happiness and even to his personal honour. He found himself
in a tragic situation, from which there was no satisfactory escape; and
there will always be many who like Fox feel that he chose wrongly.
Virgil had to celebrate the Roman Empire and the Augustan
settlement, and we have no reason for doubting that he did so willingly.
But Auden's reproach that he did not include the empire's fall in the
prophecy of Anchises is misdirected; no poet was ever more constantly
aware of the fragility and evanescence of all human things. This kind of
ambiguity is a constant feature of great art, and it is the stock-in-trade
of tragedy.

But this is only one kind of multiplicity of meaning. What kind of
multiplicity of meaning may legitimately be attributed to an author is
not a matter to be settled by *a priori* generalisation. It must depend on
the time, the place, the language, the genre and the individual nature of
the author, as well as on the character of the multiplicity of meanings
that is in question. Any critic wishing to prove a multiplicity of meanings
will have to make good his claim by detailed argument, which will need
to be subjected to most careful scrutiny. Even the greatest scholars find
it difficult to read dead authors without having their reading coloured
by the atmosphere of their own time. No Greek scholar of his day was
more learned than Wilamowitz, yet it is now easy to perceive that he
saw Euripides in terms of Ibsen. In our efforts to understand the past,
we should carry no more of our own age back with us than we can help
carrying.

Being only a classical philologist I will be mean enough to point out
that almost every time Professor Kermode quotes a Latin author he
misquotes him (see pp. 24, 115, 117, 133, and note the omission of
tantum on p. 13). The lectures are attractively presented, and contain a
wealth of information. The best thing in them is the treatment of
Hawthorne, and the detection of the influence exercised on his work
by the Harvard naturalist Louis Agassiz; did Hawthorne know of the
use made by Balzac of the work of Géoffroy de St Hilaire?

Professor Kermode reminds us that Eliot's claim for Virgil had been
anticipated by Sainte-Beuve, and rejected in favour of Homer by
Arnold in his Oxford inaugural lecture of 1860. I wish I had space to
show why I agree with Arnold that 'the classic of European literature'
is not Virgil but Homer – at any rate, the Homer of the *Iliad*.

8

The Last Days of Pompeii

The recent Pompeii exhibition has been a success in America; and this is why we are offered a handsome new edition of Bulwer-Lytton's novel, based upon one produced at the Officina Bodoni in Verona for the Limited Editions Club. Sixteen reproductions of Pompeian paintings from the catalogue of the exhibition illustrate the book; there are also some somewhat drab woodcuts by Kurt Craemer. There is a lively introduction by Edgar Johnson.

Bulwer's book first appeared in 1834, when the excavations at Pompeii and Herculaneum were the object of great interest in this country. The discovery of the buried cities was by no means new. Interesting things had been found there as early as 1607, and sporadic digging had taken place from 1689. But it was not till 1734, when Charles III of Naples became interested in the sites, that anything like serious investigation was begun, under the direction of an engineer from Spain, Rocco Gioacchino de Alcubierre. Alcubierre was interested only in treasure-hunting; eager only to find statues to decorate the royal gardens, he threw away as rubbish inscriptions splendidly incised on bronze.

From 1737 the *Philosophical Transactions* informed the British public about the discoveries; in 1748 the *Nouvelles littéraires* of the Abbé Raynal made them known in Paris. In 1758 the Chevalier de Jaucourt contributed to the *Encyclopédie* an enthusiastic article about Herculaneum and a short notice about Pompeii. Between 1757 and 1792 appeared a series of handsome volumes of the *Antichita di Ercolano*. But the encyclopaedists in general showed little interest in the discoveries. The contempt for history of the French intellectuals of the time is often exaggerated; we cannot reproach Voltaire or Montesquieu with being unhistorical. But though they had regard for 'antiquity', they had none for 'antiquities', which they despised. Montesquieu remarked that all antiquaries were charlatans, and

* A review of *The Last Days of Pompeii* by Edward George Bulwer-Lytton in *The London Review of Books*, 1979.

Voltaire in all his voluminous writings makes no mention of the buried cities. Diderot made fun of the learned Comte de Caylus:

Ci-gît un antiquaire acariâtre et brusque.
Ah! qu'il est bien logé dans cette cruche étrusque!

But if literary men were indifferent, artists were not. The baroque and the rococo were losing favour, and the cult of noble simplicity and classical austerity was spreading. The first really informed guidance to the understanding of Pompeian art came during the 1760s from Winckelmann, the first scholar to distinguish the different styles of ancient art to whose writings artists paid attention. After Vien, the representative artists of the new movement were Mengs and David; it was not from literature but from art that André Chénier learned the importance of the buried cities. His work was affected by this knowledge; so was the *Anacharsis* of the Abbé Barthélemy, published in 1788. Even women's fashions showed the influence of Pompeian art. Despite the distractions of the great wars, work at the buried cities continued; during Murat's brief reign in Naples, his wife Caroline, Napoleon's sister, did all she could to encourage excavation.

In England, too, Classicism came into fashion: this was the age of Stuart and Revett's journeys, the folios of the Society of Dilettanti and Wood's essay on the original genius of Homer. During the 1770s, Sir William Hamilton, who had personally taken part in the excavations, did much to make the new discoveries known. After England's isolation from the Continent was ended by Napoleon's defeat, interest in the buried cities heightened. Two very different poets, Shelley and the banker Samuel Rogers, were inspired by the dramatic nature of the catastrophe that had overwhelmed them. In 1817 and 1819, the dilettante archaeologist Sir William Gell published the two handsome volumes of his *Pompeiana*. He guided round the sites Sir Walter Scott, then nearing the end of his life. Like Shelley, Scott was less moved by the remains than by the thought of the destruction of the cities, and repeatedly exclaimed: 'The City of the Dead!'

Meanwhile, excavation continued to be desultory and unsystematic. A few people like Chateaubriand realised how much the sites could teach us about ancient life, particularly if the objects found there were not at once carted off to the museum; but it was not until Italy had been united under the Piedmontese dynasty that the work took on a modern and scientific aspect. By great good fortune, Giuseppe Fiorelli, already known as a numismatist, became secretary to the brother of Victor Emmanuel II and so made the acquaintance of the King, who put him in charge of the excavations. This excellent appointment was the beginning of a new era. Systematic study and excavation have continued ever since then, revealing vast quantities of information about ancient life and art; and within the last few years, a buried city, Opluntis, has been discovered. Literary scholars look on this find with somewhat mixed feelings. They would like to persuade the archaeologists to cut down through the solid lava – harder, unfortunately, than rock – in the hope of finding libraries that might contain the lost masterpieces of ancient literature. In the eighteenth century the excavators fetched up from tunnels papyri that proved to contain valuable texts relating to the Epicurean philosophy; another such library might possess Archilochus, or Ennius, or lost tragedies of Aeschylus, and Sophocles. Many of the papyrus rolls discovered long ago are carbonised, so that they have not been opened; scholars are working at a new technique for dealing with them.

Late in 1833, Gell guided round the sites the rich, well-born novelist and politician Edward George Bulwer-Lytton, with his termagant of an Irish wife. The spoiled child of a doting mother, Bulwer – he added his mother's maiden name of Lytton to his own – had had a desultory education, part of it at Cambridge, had experienced a romantic tragedy and also a brief affair with Lady Caroline Lamb; and at 29 had already published several novels. The idea of writing about Pompeii had been suggested to him by a picture he had seen in the Brera at Milan. Till now the picture's identity has remained unknown, but my colleague Robert Dingley, to whose learning this review is much indebted, has identified it as one by the Russian artist Karl Brullov; it shows, in the sentimental fashion of the time, a series of pathetic incidents during the destruction of Pompeii. A year later, Bulwer published *The Last Days of Pompeii*, which was to prove the most successful of his many works. Critics as various as Isaac D'Israeli, Felicia Hemans and Lady Blessington wrote to congratulate the author; their high opinion of the work was shared by the British public; and even in recent times the book has not been forgotten.

At that time the craze for historical novels was at its height: in his Parisian garret Lucien de Rubempré was working on *L'Archer de Charles X*, the work that was to make his fortune. Lukacs, in his study of the historical novel, argues that the best specimens were written while Hegelian ideas permeated the atmosphere. These not only depicted with real truthfulness the whole culture to which their characters belonged, but showed those characters as thinking in the fashion peculiar to their place and time. This is far harder for a novelist to achieve if he has chosen to write about the ancient world. Ancient literature is seldom colloquial and still less often confessional; the materials for writing a novel that tried to give the 'stream of consciousness' of characters in the ancient world do not exist. The only historical novel about the ancient world that I have found at all convincing is *Salammbô*; and Flaubert was wise to locate it not in Greece or Rome, of which we know a good deal, but in Carthage, of which we know little and possess no literature. Flaubert took immense trouble to get the externals right: an Italian scholar later systematically checked the details and established the novelist's accuracy beyond question. Yet the psychology even of *Salammbô* does not convince: when Sainte-Beuve pointed out the resemblance between Salammbô herself and Madame Bovary, Flaubert hardly managed to refute him.

But it is absurd to mention Flaubert in connection with the novel we are now discussing. Bulwer certainly took trouble about the details of daily life. Parts of his book remind me of the German professor, A.W. Becker, who published two books designed to illustrate the daily life of Greeks and Romans respectively in fairly full detail. He gave these works the form of novels, depicting short periods in the lives of a young Greek, Charicles, and a young Roman, Gallus, after whom the books are named; they were successful in Victorian England, in the translation of the Rev. Frederick Metcalfe. Since Becker's aims were scholarly rather than literary, it is not fair to judge him by literary standards: but I prefer his writing to that of Bulwer in the sections of his book that venture upon Becker's territory. Wishing to give a description of a Pompeian house that shall be 'as clear and unpedantic as possible', Bulwer gives us six pages about the vestibulum, the atrium, the impluvium, the tablinum, the triclinium: at the rich merchant's banquet 'the seats were veneered with tortoise-shell, and covered with quilts stuffed with feathers,' and 'the slaves showered flowers upon the couches and the floor, and covered each guest with rosy garlands, intricately woven with ribands, tied by the rind of the linden-tree, and each intermingled with the ivy and the amethyst – supposed preventives against the effect of wine.' There is a good deal more of this.

The various episodes contain reminiscences of Petronius, Juvenal, Plautus and other writers; but neither the dialogue nor the behaviour of the characters suggests a Roman atmosphere. The characters frequently exclaim 'Tush' or 'Fie'; they often swear by Pollux or by Hercules; and their speeches are sometimes interlarded with the kind of Latin phrases one remembers from the fifth form: but in general they speak the ordinary language of Victorian romantic prose, with a thick patina of archaism. 'What!' exclaims the villain, 'thinkest thou

Arbaces will brook such a rival as this puny Greek?' Even worse than
Bulwer's prose are the many poems inserted in the text; the verse is
sub-Shelleyan, with some influence from Thomas Moore.

When the element which Bulwer has in common with Becker is
abstracted, we are left with a romantic novelette of melodramatic
character, spiced with a particularly mawkish kind of Evangelical
Christianity. A rich young Greek, Glaucus, 'an Alcibiades without
ambition', falls for a Greek lady called Ione, in comparison with
whom the dreariest of Scott's young heroines seems a ball of fire.
Glaucus's rival for her affections is the Egyptian Arbaces, the Aleister
Crowley of his time, who claims descent from Rameses, dabbles in
magic, and while exploiting the charlatanism of the cult of Isis really
respects no gods but Nature and Necessity. Ione's wet brother
Apaecides falls under the Egyptian's influence and becomes a priest of
Isis, but then breaks away and becomes a Christian. Arbaces murders
him, and cunningly makes use of the hopeless passion for Glaucus of
the blind flower-seller Nydia (who bears a marked resemblance to
Little Nell) to get the innocent Glaucus convicted of the murder and
condemned to be eaten by a lion in the amphitheatre. Like that of
Androcles in the story which Shaw took from Pliny, this lion turns out
to be an amiable puss: then Glaucus is saved by the eruption of
Vesuvius, in which Arbaces perishes, crushed by the falling statue of
the Roman Emperor. The cruel and greedy loungers of Pompeii
perish, but Glaucus and Ione escape, redeemed by their conversion to
the faith of the Nazarenes; poor Nydia, however, slips away and
drowns herself.

Macaulay as an undergraduate at Trinity won the Chancellor's
Medal with a poem on Pompeii, and when his father complained that
the poem lacked a moral, replied that the subject seemed not to offer
one. Lytton found a moral where Macaulay, despite the background
of the Clapham Sect, had failed: the success of the book doubtless
owed much to its religious element. In fact, Pompeii was by no means
a mere playground for the idle rich, as modern excavations have
shown. Mr Johnson in his introduction feels obliged to say what he
can in favour of the book: but it is an uphill task. He admits that it is
full of undigested information, and that the dialogue is 'often clumsy
and unconvincing': for 'often' I would say 'always'. But he thinks the
book 'triumphs over all its deficiencies', because the applause it
earned for its 'truth to history and its vividness' is well deserved:
Bulwer has 'distilled a real vitality of understanding' from Plautus,
Terence, Horace, Catullus, Ovid, Petronius and Juvenal. Let anyone
who thinks that read three pages of Petronius and then turn to
Bulwer: it will be like starting a meal in the Tour d'Argent and

finishing it at London Airport. The descriptions of life in Pompeii, Mr Johnson finds, 'are handled not only with accuracy, but with brilliance and dash'; 'it is, indeed,' he thinks, 'one of the great reconstructions of the past.' The characters are 'clearly and sharply drawn', and most of them – though not even Mr Johnson can take Ione – are 'portrayed with a swift and unfaltering hand'. Mr Johnson praises the 'tautly mounting suspense' achieved by occasional mentions of a dark cloud hovering over Vesuvius: certainly we know the eruption will start just in time to save the hero. He finds that Bulwer's aspiration to have achieved 'a just representation of the human passions and the human heart' has been fulfilled. I prefer the products of Bulwer's spiritual descendant, Cecil B. De Mille, which are less boring and a good deal less pretentious. Landor, in a poem written when the book was new, did it perfect justice:

> If aught so damping and so dull were
> As these Last Days of Dandy Bulwer,
> And had been cast upon the pluvious
> Rockets that issued from Vesuvius,
> They would no more have reached Pompeii,
> Than Rome, or Tusculum, or Veii.

9

The Classics in Britain Today

Professor Hugh Trevor-Roper's presidential address to the Joint Association of Classical Teachers, printed in the *Spectator* for July 14, has struck some people, as you tell us, as being 'a wholesale attack on the classics'. I am by no means of this opinion; but I should like to comment on some of the remarks which it contains. Its author is not only a scholar whom I admire but a valued friend and colleague, so that I cannot be suspected of animus against him. But since he gave up classical studies in favour of historical studies in 1934, he will not be offended if a professional student of the subject suggests that he is in some details incorrect.

No classical scholar now claims for his discipline the dominating place in education which it held till well into the nineteenth century. It acquired that position, as Professor Trevor-Roper says, because people believed that the ancients furnished them with a pattern worthy of imitation. That belief depended on the assumption that their own historical position resembled, to a significant degree, the position of the ancients.

That belief survived, in certain of its forms, well into the nineteenth century; but its historical base was destroyed by the historicism of that age. The great classical scholars of the time, who were with few exceptions Germans, held that the classical civilisation was only one of many civilisations worthy of study; they studied it with particular intensity because of its special historical relation to modern Europe and because of the intrinsic interest of its history and the intrinsic value of its art and literature. To them every detail of a past civilisation seemed worth studying, because every detail contributed to the understanding of the whole; to this end, many were prepared to devote their lives to dry and arduous tasks. An eminent representative of this kind of outlook was Wilamowitz, whom I do not recognise in

---

* A letter to the Editor of the *Spectator*, which had published Hugh Trevor-Roper's address to the Joint Association of Classics Teachers (*Spectator*, 14 July 1973) in the *Spectator*, 28 July 1973.

Professor Trevor-Roper's account of him. To him Wilamowitz 'symbolises the barrenness of a purely literary and philological approach to the classics'. That is the exact opposite of the truth; nowadays Wilamowitz is sometimes criticised for having approached antiquity from a standpoint that was too exclusively historical.

The historical attitude was not, of course, confined to the classics; it pervaded the discipline of mediaeval and modern history also. The historicists' self-indulgence in the accumulation of detail was bound to arouse protest. Nietzsche complained that instead of asking, as they did, 'What can we do for scholarship?' people ought to ask, 'What can scholarship do for us?' He did not share the belief of the earlier 'classicists' that the ancients could supply us with an ideal pattern; but he sided with them against the historicists in his belief that we could learn most from antiquity by concentrating upon its greatest and most creative period and by looking not simply for its resemblances to our own civilisation as for the differences between them.

In that respect, Nietzsche started a revolution; since then the best classical scholars have been chiefly interested in those features of the ancient world which separate it from our own. It is just because the ancient world, though it was the ancestor of our own, was yet so different from it, that its study is so difficult and so rewarding.

Professor Trevor-Roper complains of the excessive interest and respect paid by scholars to the art of verbal emendation. Textual criticism seems to me more difficult and more rewarding than could be guessed from the account of it offered in a few lines of his article. Housman, it is true, chose to concentrate his great powers upon textual study according to an eighteenth-century tradition (a tradition which we may associate with Porson, but not with Bentley, a great textual critic but also a great scholar in much wider fields, and as Housman readily admitted a far more important figure in the history of scholarship than either Porson or himself). Housman has still a few imitators; but his attitude is now very far from common, and no one need fear that if he reads classics at the university he risks being condemned to an excessive quantity of this kind of work.

Professor Trevor-Roper devotes about a column to tales of the tactlessness of Eduard Fraenkel,[1] the famous German scholar who held the chair of Latin at Oxford from 1935 to 1953, and taught there for many years after his retirement. Fraenkel arrived in England after a distressing experience of racial persecution. He found things strange at first, and he was far too honest to pretend to feel immediately at home. Certainly he was often rude and tactless at this time. But

---

[1] See *Blood for the Ghosts*, ch. 21.

Fraenkel lived to become one of the most popular and successful Oxford teachers of his day. No trouble was too great for him to take on behalf of anyone who showed even the slightest interest in the classics, and even the unlikeliest people were often deeply impressed by his absolute devotion to the study of antiquity in all its branches, as it had been conceived by the great scholars of the nineteenth century, and in particular by Wilamowitz. Whatever Wilamowitz was, he was never dull or pedantic. Fraenkel's insistence on scrupulous care over details made him seem to some pedantic; but he never forgot the connection of classical studies with real life, and he communicated his attitude to his audiences.

The view of the place and prospects of their subject taken in the last section of Professor Trevor-Roper's address would be accepted by most classical scholars of the present day. It is not generally realised that, if we make exception for the towering genius of Bentley, English classical scholars have achieved more during the twentieth century than in any previous age. To name only a few, Sir John Beazley, the great authority on Greek vases, Sir Ronald Syme, the eminent historian of Rome,[2] and Mr Edgar Lobel,[3] who has published with unique skill many precious fragments of Greek literature recovered from the sands of Egypt, are surely among the most distinguished scholars of modern times. Able people who have studied at the university a course influenced by these men's work have not found the subject dull or trivial.

Why then, are classical studies so unpopular in modern England? Why are those who control the media of communication so hostile to our subject? Partly, I believe, because the twentieth century has concerned itself much with the irrational side of human nature and associated the classics with an excessive orderliness and logicality; it is significant that one of the most important books written by a living classical scholar is E.R. Dodds's *The Greeks and the Irrational*, which is well calculated to dissolve this prejudice.

There is also, I think, a social reason, and an even more superficial one; classical studies are associated in many minds with such unfashionable notions as 'the establishment', the public schools, the ruling classes. Close as it has been, the connection of classical studies with these entities hardly destroys the significance of the ancient world and its influence on the modern. Karl Marx[4] was devoted to the classics, and was profoundly influenced by his study of them, nor can

---

[2] See below, p. 74f.

[3] See *Blood for the Ghosts*, ch.1.

[4] Ibid., ch.11.

the origins of his philosophy be fully understood by those unwilling to take account of this. One could give many similar examples.

A third main reason for the unpopularity of classical studies is that they are difficult. So is any really rewarding academic discipline. Those who wish for an easy subject, and one calculated, like the old type of divinity, to strengthen their prejudices rather than to subject them to critical scrutiny, had better turn to what nowadays passes for sociology.

Every generation asks different questions about the past; and in our own time some classical scholars are asking questions about classical antiquity that anyone but an ignorant philistine can see are relevant to our own condition. The subject is difficult, and no one now claims that it should have the central place in humanistic education that it once enjoyed. But for those suited to it it offers, and will always offer, an education second to none. I know that my friend Professor Trevor-Roper will agree with me.

10

Toynbee's Greece

For Dr Toynbee a 'civilisation' is the name of the unit which he likes to isolate from the rest of history, hypostatise by means of an analogy with the human individual, and accommodate to the laws of his own peculiar compound of Hegelian determinism and Jungian theories of the collective unconscious. In this special sense, the 'Hellenic civilisation' comprises not merely the civilisation of ancient Greece, but that of the Hellenised Orient and of the Roman Empire to the time of Constantine. *Hellenism* offers a summary account of the political and military history of the Greco-Roman epoch.

Ancient Greek thought presents, on the face of it, no strikingly close resemblance to nineteenth-century English liberalism; and yet the adherents of the latter have obstinately insisted on finding its reflection in the former. Lowes Dickinson, for instance, won a considerable reputation by presenting as an account of '*the* Greek view of life' a book that tells one much about Victorian liberalism but nothing whatever about what it professes to describe. It is not specially interesting to read yet another account of Hellenism written from a Victorian liberal point of view; but one must be grateful to the author for not having allowed a belief in the liberal myth about the Greeks to prevent his natural aversion to almost everything about them from being perceptible.

Dr Toynbee scolds the Greeks severely for not having united during the fifth century. Once they missed that chance, they were done for; 'the nemesis of this failure was the international and civil warfare that devastated the Hellenic world, with hardly a breathing-space, for four hundred years.' He allows that after that Augustus managed to re-establish some kind of order; 'but the wounds that Hellenism had already inflicted on itself were lethal.' It is odd that the same writer should so strongly disapprove of Periclean Athens for having made the one serious attempt to unify Greece before the time of Philip. If the

* A review of *Hellenism: History of a Civilisation* by A.J. Toynbee in the *Spectator*, 1 May 1959.

Athenians had resisted the temptation to turn the Delian league into an empire, Dr Toynbee says, 'the economic tide making for closer political union' would probably have kept the league in being; and it would eventually have led to 'some kind of voluntary political unification of the Hellenic world as a whole'. Had the Greek city states been dominated by enlightened liberal manufacturers of the Manchester School, Dr Toynbee's surmise would undoubtedly be correct; and yet all we know of these communities, with their jealous passion for independence, suggests that the only feasible means of unifying them at that date lay in the use of force. But Dr Toynbee has assured us in a later work that no institution based on the use of force can have any permanent importance.

Like many previous writers, Dr Toynbee grossly exaggerates the destructive consequences of the Peloponnesian War. It is true that in that war Athens lost her one real chance of uniting Greece under her own leadership. But her own recovery, and that of the other belligerents, was remarkably rapid; there is really much more to be said for the fourth century and even for the Hellenistic Age, than Dr Toynbee will allow. To read his brief and superficial summary, one would suppose the whole history of the Mediterranean world from Aegospotami to Actium was one unrelieved stretch of disaster and decline. Dr Toynbee lectures the pupils in this dismal academy with all the firmness of a well-informed and intelligent housemaster, liberal in the best sense, whose high Anglicanism has been softened by memories of a nonconformist background into a vague sympathy with all 'higher' forms of theism. At every crisis, he knows what would have been the only reasonable thing to do; he answers every question of right and wrong with the same unhesitating assurance. He makes war and politics, as well as morals, seem childishly simple.

Take Dr Toynbee's attitude to the greatest and most complex problem of ancient history, that of accounting for the decline of the Empire. He seems to take it for granted that this was due mainly to internal decay, and says little of external factors. Yet whoever looks at a map and compares the territory of the Empire with the vast areas occupied by the barbarians outside it must wonder not so much that the Empire fell as that it survived for anything like the time it did. Rome came near to destruction by the Cimbri; and later in the century Julius Caesar probably forestalled a similar threat. Perhaps the greatest achievement of Augustus was his stabilisation of the northern frontiers: a work in which his record of unbroken success was spoiled, late in his life, by the disaster of Varus, an event that carried the most sinister omen for the future.

Like most historians, Dr Toynbee holds that an important factor in the collapse of the Empire was the decline of the Hellenic middle class; but the reasons that he gives for this are neither exhaustive nor convincing. He insists that the middle class was unable to feel towards a larger unit the same loyalty it had felt towards a city state; and he says little of the appalling burdens laid on that class by the fiscal and administrative policy of Diocletian and his successors. One is left wondering how so good a liberal would react to the suggestion that one of the numerous and complicated reasons why the Empire fell may have been that it tried to offer too many privileges to too many of its subjects.

But despite his great store of varied information, Dr Toynbee is above all a historian of ideas; and among the reasons he gives for the decline we must expect ideas to bulk larger than mere brute facts. Hellenism seems to have been doomed from the start; for in the first chapter we are told that it was the first great civilisation to 'put its treasure' in 'Humanism, or Man-Worship.' The Olympian religion Dr Toynbee says, was a mere deification of barbarian humanity; belief in it, weak even in Homer's time, died out as early as the fifth and fourth centuries, to be replaced officially by state-worship and the cults of deified rulers. The deficiencies of these beliefs could scarcely be made good by the Orphic and Pythagorean cults, the mystery religions or the superstition of astrology, nor by the abstract religions excogitated by philosophers. All these are merely stages in the collapse of Hellenism and the inevitable triumph of the Church of Christ.

It is hard for the adherent of one religion to enter in imagination into the standpoint of another, or to see it as anything but an absurd superstition or a primitive groping towards the truth which he himself knows. It does not easily come home to him that the attitude of other men towards their divinities may not be the same as his own to his. Many modern scholars find it hard to accept, despite much evidence to the contrary, that the Greeks ever believed in the Olympian gods; both their numbers and their character seem to disqualify them as objects of genuine religious feeling. Yet a candid inquirer may well concede that, on a superficial view, many features of life on this planet are more easily explained on a polytheistic than on a monotheistic hypothesis. To take a mythological example, both Artemis and Aphrodite are powers to be reckoned with, and if like Hippolytus we lean too far towards the one, we may easily have trouble with the other. Moreover, to call Olympianism 'man-worship' is monstrously unjust. No religion has insisted more firmly on the distinction between god and man, or has reminded its adherents oftener that they must remember the limitations of their mortal status. This attitude lies near the root of all the Greek art and literature of the greatest period; failure to sympathise with it has led, more than any other cause, to failure to understand that art.

For such a religious attitude to continue in existence, it is not necessary that its deities should continue to be believed in with the simplicity of an age of faith. Belief in the gods could become little more than formal without the essential attitude becoming modified; for even during the age of faith, the believer had been taught that the gods ruled the universe for their own sake, not for man's, and that their actions were for the most part incomprehensible to men. Thus religious belief conflicted only in the mildest way with the growth of philosophy, no particular body of dogmas having acquired a sanction that it was sacrilege to challenge. But not everyone could be tough enough to continue without the prop of some kind of supernatural agency, particularly when so many Oriental religions were at hand to offer such support. Even during the fifth century such beliefs had become influential; in the vast melting-pot of the Hellenistic world their importance grew; and once the barbarians had become necessary to the survival of the Empire, the time when it must make an ally of one or another of the dogmatic religions could not be long delayed.

Dr Toynbee's utter lack of sympathy with the Greek religious outlook lies, it seems to me, at the root of his dislike for the civilisation he has described. He seems to think the Hellenic civilisation perished at some time during the fourth century after Christ; but he allows that there have since occurred 'periodic eruptions' of the 'explosive Hellenic spirit' that lies buried beneath the surface, one of which was the Renaissance. The patronising distaste which pervades this facile and superficial summary must arouse the annoyance of those who still try to continue the tradition of independent thinking which this 'eruption' set in motion. But they must still thank Dr Toynbee for not having pretended to like things he obviously neither approves of nor, for all his knowledge, understands.

11

The Virtues of a Literary Culture

In the thirties the great benefactor of classical studies in this country was Adolf Hitler, who gained for us the services of a group of distinguished scholars from the Continent. Beside his colossal statue we should erect a smaller one to Senator Joseph MacCarthy, without whom Professor M.I. Finley might not have left America in the 'fifties and moved to Cambridge. Since then he has been a vital force in the study of ancient history in this country, never more than during the last year, when he has published a learned and original study of *The Ancient Economy*, a stimulating small book *Democracy: Ancient and Modern*, and now a collection of twelve essays, which are as good as, if not better than, anything he has done before. They make an important contribution to scholarship which is also of great interest and value to the general reader; and like all Professor Finley's works they deserve to be and will be widely read.

Professor Finley tells us that the echo in his title of Nietzsche's essay 'On the Use and Disadvantage of History' is not an accident; and although he is no Nietzschian – the only false statement I have found in the book is the claim (pp. 193-4) that Nietzsche was a German nationalist[1] – he writes history in a way that satisfies most of Nietzsche's requirements. In the past ancient history in England has too often taken the form of what Nietzsche calls 'monumental history,' which as he says quickly slides into mythical fiction. Large parts of the *Cambridge Ancient History* (I am not referring to the new edition) seems to me to fall within this category; one of its main editors, Professor Finley's Cambridge predecessor Sir Frank Adcock, has always supplied me with my mental picture of Isocrates, who is not Professor Finley's favourite ancient author.

Ancient history too often took the form of a bland continuous

* A review of *The Uses and Abuses of History* by M.I. Finley in the *Spectator*, 1 March 1975.

[1] I ought to say that in a letter to me written after the publication of this review Sir Moses Finley retracted this statement.

narrative, its tone and interests dictated by those of the Greek and Roman historians themselves; the questions that a modern student of history, politics or social life would ask were not raised by scholars ignorant of the modern world to which they were supposed to be interpreting the ancient. Another defect of English ancient historians in the past is closely allied with one of the principal advantages they have enjoyed, that of receiving a sound literary and linguistic training. Many of them have been too busy with textual exposition, epigraphy and other ancilliary disciplines to give proper attention to the actual subject-matter of ancient history and to the problems which it poses to the modern student. An historian singularly free from both these defects is Arnaldo Momigliano, to whom this book is dedicated and to whose work one of the essays is devoted.

Professor Finley is above all else a critical historian, alert to diagnose and to attack a problem; he rightly argues that history without generalisations is no history at all. His keen intelligence is specially effective where scepticism is needed. He has already done valuable work in resisting the temptation to exaggerate the historical element contained in the Homeric epics; and now he rightly questions the assumption, made even by great scholars, of a general unity underlying the diversity of the Greek legal systems. He points out that we have no reason to suppose that the main features of the Spartan system were earlier than the sixth century, and that the origins of some of the customs that played a part in it are hardly relevant to their functions. He reminds us how little the later Greeks cared to follow Herodotus and Thucydides in writing critical history, and how little they thought of themselves as a nation. Ready as he is to make use of other disciplines to illuminate his own, his attitude to them is never unwary. In discussing the relevance of anthropology (and sociology) to the classics he argues that functional anthropology is insufficiently sensitive to the element of change; this is true, but in the past classical scholars have so exaggerated the 'development' of ancient society and culture that Lévi-Strauss's insistence that the synchronic picture must not be obscured by the diachronic has its value. In a paper about archaeology in relation to history Professor Finley deals condignly with arbitrary guesses about early religion based on archaeological data, but at the same time makes an equally justified protest against the tendency to seal off archaeology as an independent discipline forming a private preserve for archaeologists; and he supports his protest by giving examples of the kind of data useful to historians which archaeologists often will not trouble to provide. His familiarity with modern as well as ancient history is nowhere more in evidence than in the brilliant inaugural lecture given at Cambridge in 1970, where he compares the assertion, common in fifth-century Athens, that the Athenians must either conserve or return to their 'ancestral constitution' with the use of corresponding legends of 'the Saxon customs' and 'Jeffersonian democracy' in the England of the early Stuarts and the America of the New Deal.

I come lastly to two essays with which my sympathy is less complete. An excellent survey of ancient Utopias, drawing some necessary distinctions and, in particular, marking them off from Golden Ages, is rounded off with a page or two on modern Utopianism. This Professor Finley complains, has become paralysed; now that technology removes the material difficulties that stand in the way of the establishment of Utopias, the difficulties raised by 'the burdens of fear and guilt, of domination,' seem more formidable than before. He feels sad that modern Utopias tend to be Dystopias (Huxley, Orwell); he does not mention that one or two actual attempts to bring the thing off do not seem to all of us to have been complete successes. A reference to Popper might have been in place here; the collection *Conjectures and Refutations* actually contains a paper called 'Utopias and Violence'.

The last essay in the book is called 'The Heritage of Isocrates'. Professor Finley complains that for two thousand years higher education has been centred upon literary culture; as modern advocates of this dispensation he cites E.R. Curtius and F.R. Leavis, but as I read the chapter I could not help thinking of Sir Frank Adcock. Professor Finley argues that this state of affairs 'is no longer firmly grounded in the social structure and its institutional arrangements'; it seems a pity that his indication of the measures he would take is crowded into half a page at the very end. 'First,' he writes, 'the range and variety of experience, literary, philosophical, historical, scientific, which schooling contributes to the equipment of the student must be enlarged and correlated so as to be adequate to life in a democratic society of great technical complexity, improving material satisfaction and increasing free time.' For this purpose education is to be continued 'into the early years of intellectual, emotional and social maturity'; also, the past is to be deconsecrated and converted into a living, a *relevant* past.

I find here a certain vagueness; but it seems certain that Professor Finley's statement would not to be found fault with by, and might even encourage, those who would make a training like that given by the University of Essex compulsory for all. It seems certain, too, that he would like to see literary and linguistic education much curtailed In America, where Rousseauite reluctance to make children work has been propagated by the powerful influence of John Dewey, few children are taught languages at the age at which the memory is best; the resulting ignorance seems to me in many ways unfortunate. Even in historical study, to say nothing of other studies or of life in general, languages, literature, and the history of religion and metaphysics have something to contribute.

Historians who are as sensitive to these departments of life as Syme or Trevor-Roper, and like them are themselves distinguished writers in a literary sense, command not only an instrument of communication but an instrument of historical understanding which is not at the disposal of historians who, however, keen and searching their intelligence and however clear and concise their style, have been denied or have failed to develop this particular gift. Apart from whatever value it may have for its own sake, Greek and Roman literature played such an important part in the life and politics of its time that it is specially important to historians. Even the general student of antiquity must take adequate account of this, and no general survey which fails to do so can be recommended without reserve. The fox who had lost his tail in a trap tried to persuade all the other foxes to cut off their tails also. We know that there are very fine foxes without tails, and that is lucky, since before long the tails of all fox-cubs will be amputated in the name of social justice. But until then we shall not allow even the most eloquent of tailless foxes to persuade us to cut off our own.

12

The Limits of Hellenisation

The most learned ancient historian, perhaps the most learned historian in the western world, who since retiring from his London chair has moved between Pisa, Chicago, and All Souls College, Oxford, has made of lectures given first at Cambridge and later at Bryn Mawr a small book which is not only one of the finest specimens of his scholarship, but is also written with elegance, clarity and wit. It deals with the rewarding topic of the cultural connections of the Greeks with Romans, Celts, Jews and Iranians during the Hellenistic period. Carthage is left out because too little is known about it, the Romans having destroyed the city in 146 BC; Egypt is left out because the Greeks had recognised the importance of its culture well before the Hellenistic age.

The book brings out with startling clarity the lack of interest shown by the Greeks in all civilisations but their own. The astonishing enterprise that, during the eighth and seventh centuries BC, led them to plant their colonies over the whole Mediterranean coastline from the Black Sea to Gibraltar did not extend to an eagerness to understand the thinking of the foreigners with whom they came into contact. The great city of Massalia (Marseilles), founded by the Asiatic Greek city of Phocaea about 600 BC, would have made an excellent base for expeditions into the interior of Gaul to carry out researches. No such expeditions were sent out. The Greeks preferred to sail along the coast, and seldom entered the interior which so many of their products penetrated. During the fourth century Pytheas sailed to this country and to Jutland, but had nothing to report about inland France itself. Even when the Gauls invaded Greece and established a principality in Asia Minor, Greek art might depict them but Greek writers ignored them – until a century later the Roman ruling class required them to satisfy its demand for description and interpretation.

The first serious efforts to describe Gaul and Spain were made by

* A review of *Alien Wisdom: The Limits of Hellenisation* by Arnaldo Momigliano in the *Spectator*, 3 January 1976.

the historian Polybius (*c*.201-120 BC); unfortunately most of the parts of his work that contained them have been lost. We know more of the subsequent description by the great Stoic philosopher, Posidonius (*c*.135-51 BC). Troubled at first by the sight of human heads nailed up outside the houses of the Gallic chiefs, this brilliant cosmopolitan intellectual familiarised himself with that alien culture, and his highly intelligent and readable account of the Celts was useful to Julius Caesar while he was conquering Gaul. Polybius and Posidonius were also the chief contributors to Greek understanding of a more important foreign people, the Romans, although Greek influence in Rome had been powerful from an early date. Rome was long ruled by the Etruscans, a people deeply, though selectively, influenced by Greek culture; and throughout the present century research has made it ever clearer that Greek influence in Italy began earlier and went deeper than had previously been realised. During the third century BC, Rome became imbued with Greek culture. She created a new literature of her own upon a Greek basis, written, to begin with, by Greeks or by Italians from Greek-speaking areas. We now know that a passage of Plautine comedy full of Greek touches is not necessarily a translation from the Greek original, because Plautus himself was steeped in the Greek atmosphere. The legend that Cato learned Greek at eighty is absurd; not only does his treatise on agriculture depend on Greek handbooks,[1] but in his time leading Romans often spoke the language of international diplomacy. The first Roman historian was the aristocrat Fabius Pictor, who wrote in Greek.

From the time of the defeat of the great Greek commander Pyrrhus by the Romans about 280 BC, the Greeks had to take serious account of Rome. The Ptolemies were in touch with her; the Sicilian historian Timaeus (*c*.346-250 BC) gave much information about her. During the second century BC, when Rome became the dominant power inside Greece itself, Greek interest in her naturally increased. Polybius lived in Rome as a hostage from 167, and became intimate with the younger Scipio and with other leading Romans. He described the Roman aristocracy and the institutions upon which its strength depended; Posidonius, superior in intelligence and in literary skill, continued his work. The importance of their presentation of Rome has been generally recognised; Momigliano, following in the tracks of Mommsen, now reminds us of its limitations. Deceived by the superficial similarity of Rome to a Hellenic polis – the philosopher Heraclides Ponticus had called her that as early as the fourth century BC – they failed to look at her through the ethnological telescope

---

[1] See S. Boscherini, *Lingua e scienza greca nel 'De agricultura' di Catone* (1970).

which gave Polybius so clear a view of Alexandria and Posidonius of the Celts. They failed to perceive the radical differences that separated the Romans from themselves. Neither described the workings of the military system as it affected Rome's Italian allies, or recognised the need to keep the allies busy by constant war that drew Rome irresistibly into her career of conquest. Mommsen, Momigliano reminds us, saw the superficiality of Polybius' theory that Rome had a 'mixed constitution' and that her success was due to this.

Greek contacts with the Jews began earlier; King David employed Cretan archers, Cretans or Carians fought for Joash in the ninth century, and Greek pottery existed at Samaria during the eighth. Greek connections with Egypt and with Persia brought about connections with Judaea. Yet the Jews are not mentioned in classical Greek literature; only after Alexander did the Greeks take account of their existence. Jewish writings mention the Greeks as early as the seventh century, but take serious account of them only after Alexander, when Palestine came under Greek control. During the third century it was part of the Ptolemaic kingdom, and many Jews settled in Alexandria; in 198 BC it passed to the Seleucids. The Jews of Alexandria not only translated their scriptures, but created a whole literature in Greek, poetry as well as prose – we have fragments of two epics and a tragedy on early Jewish history – in order to explain their history and religion. The Greeks remained indifferent. Ptolemy Philadelphus did not really command the making of the Septuagint, nor did the Greeks read it or any of the Greek literature the Jews produced. From the fourth century the Greeks were aware that the Jews had a singular religion, and credited them with being philosophers; but they showed no real curiosity about their institutions: the conflict between the Jews and the Seleucid monarchy during the sixties of the second century was partly due to this incomprehension. At this time and later there was a considerable Hellenising party among the Jews, but this did not succeed in informing the Greeks about Jewish institutions, and Hellenism among the Jews continued to be on the surface. The Jews learned too little and too late about the Romans; and the Greeks, who might have informed each of these peoples about the other, did not attempt the task.

From the middle of the sixth century, when the Persian Empire advanced to the shores of the Aegean, the Greeks were in direct contact with the Persians. In our time two distinguished scholars, Walter Burkert and Martin West, have argued strongly for the influence of Persian religion upon early Greek philosophy; but as Momigliano warns us the theory is by no means established. The

Greeks hardly maintained the promise of an understanding of the Persians shown by the history of Herodotus. Their victories over Persia in 480-79 BC bred contempt for 'barbarians'; the accounts of Persia given by fourth-century Greeks who had good opportunities to understand its culture, like Ctesias and Xenophon, remain superficial. Plato and Aristotle show little interest in Persian history and institutions, and Momigliano is wisely cautious about what is alleged to be an Arabic version of a letter from Aristotle to Alexander recommending the deportation of the Persian aristocracy in aid of the establishment of a universal state. The influence of Zoroastrian thought on Plato has been believed in by four great scholars; yet Plato's dualism and respect for the Sun can be explained without this supposition. Momigliano rightly says that in later Greek thought the name of Zoroaster, like that of Hermes Trismegistus (identified with the Egyptian god Thoth), attracted any kind of speculation relating to astrology, the after-life or the mysteries of nature. The Greeks could not read Persian texts, and there were no translations; they were at the mercy of forgeries, of which there was no lack. From the foundation of the Parthian empire about the middle of the third century BC there were Greeks living under Parthian rule. Some of them tried to explain Parthian history and customs to their compatriots, and after the defeat of Carrhae the Romans paid attention to their writings; but the Greeks took little interest.

Greek culture had grown up without the need to study any foreign language, and the great Greek writers had the advantage given to Shakespeare by his little Latin and less Greek. To learn a foreign language must have been very difficult indeed for any Greek. Their obstinate refusal to take account of Roman literature is an astonishing fact of cultural history; only during the last few years has it been established that Greek poets even as late as the fourth and fifth centuries AD knew Latin poetry. The modern case that most illuminates the problem is surely that of the French. There have of course been periods when French culture has undergone strong foreign influence. But relatively few French people find it easy to speak a foreign language; most pay for the immense advantage of being French the price of being enclosed in a wholly French way of thought and feeling. The ancients used to say that life was tolerable neither with women nor without them. Perhaps life is tolerable neither if you are not nor if you are French. A Roman might have said that about the Greeks, with better reason.

13

Greek Popular Morality

The best study of Greek word order; the best commentary on a play of
Aristophanes (*The Clouds*) and the best introduction to Aristophanic
comedy; part of the best commentary on Thucydides and a masterly
short sketch of that writer; the proof that the authorship of a number
of surviving speeches by Greek orators is wholly uncertain; a school
edition of Theocritus that no expert can afford to neglect. All these
things stand to the credit of K.J. Dover, who in scholarly achievement
leads the Hellenists of his generation in this country. To the general
reader, at least, *Greek Popular Morality in the Time of Plato and Aristotle* is
more important than any of these, for it makes a contribution of
fundamental importance to the understanding of Greek ethics. All
quotations appear in accurate and felicitous translation; ethical terms
are given in Greek written in English letters but are never left
unexplained.

Most existing studies of Greek ethics have been based upon poetry
or philosophy; some take into account law and legal arguments.
Professor Dover has made a new departure by basing his study on an
investigation of the ethical presuppositions revealed by the writers of
the 150 or so Athenian political and forensic speeches that we possess.
He has made use of comedy, including some specimens of the New
Comedy which strictly speaking fall outside his period; he has made a
limited use of tragedy, and a very little use of epitaphs. He covers the
period between the birth of Plato in 428 BC and the death of Aristotle
in 322 BC; nearly all the evidence is Athenian. He has renounced the
use of law and legal concepts, of poetry before his period and of the
philosophers. Since philosophy is *ex hypothesi* non-popular, this choice
is justified. Yet there are some places where he might have admitted
evidence from a philosopher, especially Aristotle, who is so much
closer to ordinary Greek ethics than Plato; when he tells us that he has
failed to find in his period evidence for the existence of youthful

* A review of *Greek Popular Morality in the Time of Plato and Aristotle* by K.J. Dover in
The Times Literary Supplement, 14 March 1975.

idealism, a reference to the famous characterisation of young men in the second book of Aristotle's *Rhetoric* might have been in place.

But the general excellence of this plan is evident, since speeches addressed to political assemblies or to large citizen juries, and plays, particularly comedies, performed at public festivals before large audiences may safely be assumed to appeal to moral notions which the majority of ordinary people find acceptable. The advantage gained by this initial choice of method is made greater still by Professor Dover's familiarity with the whole body of his material, the care he always takes to bear in mind the entire context of a passage he makes use of, and the rare honesty and intelligence used in making his deductions. The clarity of the style reflects the precision of the thought; and though the structure of the book requires some effort to grasp, the contents can be mastered with comparatively little difficulty. The clarity has not been attained at the price of over-simplification; where, as so often, two or more attitudes to the same question are found among the sources, Professor Dover can be trusted to give each of them its due. There are few footnotes and not many references to other books; and yet this is a work of consummate learning.

The first chapter lists the sources and explains how they should be interpreted, and the second examines the vocabulary used to express moral notions; the remaining four classify moral attitudes according to the various factors by which they are conditioned. To know where a particular phenomenon is treated one must study the table of contents at the beginning and be ready to supplement it by using the index. Professor Dover never falls into the trap of studying words but not things; and he never makes the mistake of studying Greek morality purely in its own terms. We find answered here the questions we, as modern readers, want to ask.

These questions are answered from a point of view more sympathetic to the Greeks than that of several recent studies. It does not matter if an inferior writer judges and condemns the Greeks from the standpoint of a somewhat simple evangelical Christianity; Arthur W.H. Adkins, in a review which fails to do this book justice (*CP* 73 (1978), 143ff.), seems to survey them from the fixed base of a dogmatic Kantianism. Professor Dover is not so innocent, as he tells us in the preface, as to advocate a return to 'Hellenism'; but he clearly believes that Greek ethics contain much that is of value, and thinks an understanding of the subject can be of practical use to us in the shaping of our own attitudes. He offers no general summary of the characteristics that most differentiate the ethics of the Greeks from those of others; but he often compares Greek with Christian and with other modern attitudes, often to the advantage of the former. He reminds us that what is nowadays taken to be Christian doctrine is often very unlike the doctrine of the Gospels, or even of the Church until comparatively recent times. Not all Christian readers will be pleased at being reminded of what Christ actually said about divorce (Matthew v. 27-32 and xix, 1-12), or at being told that strife between their own sects has been the product of distinctive features of their own religion.

Professor Dover does not relate the ethical attitudes of the Greeks to the religion and world outlook that lie behind them. Yet the ethical attitudes that he reveals seem to me very much those that might have been expected in a civilisation grounded on the religion delineated in my book *The Justice of Zeus*. That book has scandalized some readers, accustomed as good liberals to concentrate on the development of Greek civilisation, because of its emphasis on the static element. I doubt whether Professor Dover is scandalized; he can speak of 'the slow pace at which Athenian society evolved'. He is perfectly aware (and so am I) that from one point of view, the pace at which Athenian civilisation evolved during the fifth and fourth centuries may be thought rapid; yet in the context which he speaks in he is entirely right.

How, then, are Greek ethics different from those of other peoples? First, the attitude of the Homeric hero who wished to excel others and to win honour during life and fame after it continues to be maintained, after a fashion, by any person of proper self-respect, even in the age of Athenian democracy. So far from turning the other cheek, the ordinary Greek, even during the fourth century, wished to benefit his friends and harm his enemies. In the name of his city he might risk his life in a fight to protect the interests of his neighbour; but he did not love his neighbour as himself, and he would not have recognised as neighbour any who was not a fellow-citizen, or at least a Greek. Like other Greeks the Athenians assigned the greatest importance to the rule of law; but they assumed that without the law each man would pursue his own self-interest, so that failures and misfits had no excuse to hold up their hands in horror at the successes won by others. Professor Dover does not quote Burckhardt, but he is well aware of the importance of contests and competitions in Greek life which Burckhardt, perhaps following Nietzsche, so strongly emphasised.

Yet Professor Dover is also well aware, as some recent students of the subject have not been, that even in the earlier Greek documents we know the uninhibited self-seeking of human beings is already restrained not only by political and social sanctions, but by ethical doctrines closely linked with a religious belief. Even in early times the general terms of ethical commendation which applied originally, and still frequently apply, to goodness in war may also imply goodness of another sort; even in early times military virtues are not the only virtues which we find commended. Not only shame but guilt also is important in Greek ethics, even in the Homeric poems. The chief demand made of men by gods not primarily interested in human welfare was indeed that they shall pay the honour due to them; but from an early date the supreme god demanded as part of the honour due to him that men be just towards one another.

There was, it is true, by no means the same certainty about the consequences of evil-doing that has prevailed in Christian societies. Zeus was thought in the end to punish the evil-doer, if not in his own person, then in those of his descendants. The purpose of the gods, and particularly of Zeus, was thought of as inscrutable; apparently inexplicable deaths and disasters might be due to an inherited guilt of which even the victims themselves were unaware.

We can trace during the historical period the rise of the belief that in the next world the dead were rewarded or punished by the gods; but not all men held this opinion, and not all who did were agreed about the nature of the divine judgment. The gods were not merciful, and faith and hope were not virtues, but attitudes that might lead to disaster. The gods were just; but their justice did not hold out to mankind the sort of comfort Christianity would later offer. Greece is a country where man finds it desperately hard to make a living, and Greek religion and ethics make for hardness. Professor Dover finds that during the period he examines Greeks were already aiming at the self-sufficiency and invulnerability to fortune later pursued by the great philosophical systems of the Hellenistic age.

The Greeks credited their gods with terrible power, yet felt that provided one did not provoke them one could maintain a friendly, though in most cases a distant, relationship. Men did not blame the gods for ruling the universe in their own interest and not in men's; but men had their own dignity, and on occasion might show greater magnanimity than gods. They did not feel it necessary to prostrate themselves in abject submission to the divine will like Orientals, at least before Plato. Great heroes were prone to run the risk of seeming to compete with gods and so suffer annihilation, demonstrating their heroism in the very moment of destruction. Ordinary men judged themselves by less exalted standards; they constantly praised 'safe thinking' – a basic rendering of the term *sōphrosynē* that is often more helpful than the renderings 'prudence' or 'moderation'. Men had to bear in mind the limitations attached to the human condition; they could draw comfort from remembering that they shared these with many others. Between the extremes of Manichaean belief in the wickedness of the world and the fatuous self-complacency of Rousseauite utopian optimism they in their notion of humanity steered a middle course.

Greek ethics were in general more intellectualist than ours. Actions were judged not by the intentions of the doers but by their results. No Greek would have said 'Be good, sweet maid, and let who will be clever'; the Greeks were not tolerant of the well-meaning idiot. Professor Dover brings this out with full force, yet rightly warns against thinking that the Greek intellectualisation of virtue was complete. The Greeks understood that one might know what one ought to do, but be prevented by one's emotions from acting on one's knowledge; Euripides' Medea and Phaedra provide classic instances. Illness, madness or erotic passion, which they conceived of as an illness, might carry one away.

Professor Dover believes that Christian attitudes have distorted the view taken of Greek notions about moral responsibility by modern scholars, including some who cannot be accused of conscious Christian bias. Belief in eternal punishment, he argues, combined with belief in divine justice has caused Christians to demand that no man should be punished for an action for which he can claim not to be morally responsible, and therefore to demand a high degree of certainty in the assignment of such responsibility. This attitude has affected the attitude of modern law-courts, which are often conceived not so much as protecting society as dealing with the prisoner as his good or bad conduct merits.

Athenian juries, he points out, seem to have cared less about the moral guilt or innocence of the defendant than about the good or bad results for the community that will follow from his condemnation or acquittal. The Greeks, he thinks, were far less confident about assigning moral responsibility than we tend to be; and since the concepts of determinism and free-will were not formulated, even by philosophers, before the Hellenistic age, many of the considerations that play a part in modern discussions of this topic were for them not operative.

Every reader of Greek forensic speeches must be struck by the attitude of Greek juries which Professor Dover here describes; at times one is even reminded of the proceedings of 'people's' courts behind the iron curtain. But, as Professor Dover himself points out, the guilt or innocence of the accused is by no means a matter of indifference; sometimes a speaker warns the jury against neglecting this factor in its eagerness to bring in the verdict most beneficial to the Athenian people. Morality was certainly one factor in the decisions of the courts; here, as in other places, the gods might be said to be its guardians. Even the law of the demos was subordinate to the divine law, as the countrymen of the author of the *Antigone* did not forget. But it is even more important to bear in mind that even if a man was not held *morally* responsible for his actions, he was still held responsible for them.

In Homer a human action is often prompted by a god, and a man who has come to regret something he has done may 'save face', as Agamemnon does in his apology to Achilles in the nineteenth book of the *Iliad*, by claiming that the god and not he is responsible. But in such cases the man cannot avoid the consequences of his act; the god's share in responsibility does not annihilate that of the human author. Professor Dover has argued (in the *Hellenic Journal* for 1973) that scholars have overrated the importance of moral responsibility in Aeschylus's *Agamemnon*. But whatever degree of guilt may attach to Agamemnon personally, there can be no doubt that the guilt inherited from his father Atreus is the determining factor in his miserable end; even if Agamemnon is not guilty, he is responsible, and his responsibility has a moral element.

If law and justice are to be maintained, human beings have to regard themselves as being responsible for their actions, whatever doubts and uncertainties may attach to their efforts to determine guilt in any given case. Yet a powerful movement starting in the eighteenth century and reaching its climax in our own time seeks to weaken or abolish the concept of responsibility; its attempt to blame 'society' for crime is reinforced by the use of psychology to beg moral questions. The Greeks were better aware of the difficulty of fixing moral responsibility than the adherents of dogmatic systems have allowed themselves to be. Yet their insistence that a man must be held responsible for his actions, whether or not he is guilty in the sense in which we use the word, is not further from Christianity than it is from Rousseauism.

14

Revolution in Roman History

During the fifty years that have elapsed since the publication of the earliest of the essays collected in these volumes, there has been a revolution in the study of Roman history in which Sir Ronald Syme has played a part comparable with that of Augustus in the revolution which his most famous book describes. When his career began, that study was still dominated by the gigantic figure of Theodor Mommsen, who was born in 1817 and died in 1903, the year of Syme's birth. The *History of Rome* which made Mommsen familiar to the general reader – it even earned him one of the earliest Nobel Prizes for Literature – was only one item in Mommsen's vast output, and was viewed by him with some misgiving as a popularising work. More important, in his view, were his detailed studies of the Roman provinces, his immense contribution to the collection and publication of inscriptions, his planning of the great series of *Monumenta Germaniae Historica*, his comprehensive works on Roman public and private law. Mommsen began from the study of Roman private law, a fact that had great consequences. For all his power to portray individuals, he was above all a student of institutions. The flaw in his approach to history was that it was too legalistic. 'He codified Roman law more than the Romans ever did,' writes Arnaldo Momigliano, 'instead of trying to see how the Roman ruling class built the system of their own government to ensure order in the State and continuity to their own rule.'

Mommsen's influence lasted long, particularly in England, where the 'Whig' approach to modern history had its counterpart in the study of Rome. The political strife of the last century of the Republic was seen in terms of a struggle between a conservative party of Optimates and a reforming party of Populares, behind whom lurked the Whigs and Tories; material seeming to support this view was furnished by the works of Cicero. The great reforming leader was the

---

* A review of *Roman Papers* by Sir Ronald Syme, edited by E. Badian, in the *London Review of Books*, November 1979.

dictator Caesar, the hero of Mommsen's *Römische Geschichte*; his heir and successor was Augustus, the restorer and reformer of the Republic. Eduard Meyer, in a famous book published in 1922, preferred to make Augustus the successor not of Caesar but of Pompeius Magnus, whom he saw as a military leader who respected the constitution.

As an undergraduate reading Greats just after the war, I attended and admired a course of twenty-four lectures on the development of the Roman constitution given by H.M. Last, Syme's predecessor in the Camden Chair of Roman history. Last had a legal cast of mind; with much learning and with subtle reasoning, he outlined the constitutional niceties of tribunician power and *imperium maius* by which Augustus justified his domination. But after I had read *The Roman Revolution*, which Syme had published in 1939, at the age of thirty-six, I felt the subject of Last's course to be a good deal less important than I had thought at first.

Born in New Zealand in 1903, Syme came to England as a Rhodes Scholar. He started as a military historian; his first large undertaking was to write for the tenth volume of the Cambridge Ancient History (1934) an admirable account of Rome's northern frontiers from the start of Augustus' reign to the end of that of Nero. This work must have impressed on him the central importance of the fact that after Actium Augustus controlled all the legions; compared with that, tribunician power and *imperium maius* mattered little. Living in the thirties, and hearing Mussolini haranguing the mob from the balcony of the Palazzo Venezia, Syme would appear to have reached the conclusion that constitutional niceties, fascinating as they were, signified less than the realities of power.

'The policy and acts of the Roman People,' he wrote in the masterly opening chapters of *The Roman Revolution*, in which he sketched his own approach, 'were guided by an oligarchy, its annals were written in an oligarchic spirit.' He set himself to study that oligarchy in detail, observing the local origins of its members, their connections by blood and marriage, the details of their careers. To this task he brought a sovereign command of the literary texts and numerous inscriptions which furnished his material. He knows the Latin language and literature better than most professors of Latin, and has a delicate feeling for the nuances of style; starting from the pioneer work on Roman proper names of the great comparative linguist Wilhelm Schulze, he knows how to extract historical information from the observation that a particular name points to a particular Italian region. He takes nothing for granted; in the handling of his sources, his critical sense is never not alert. Every person and every problem is grasped in its concrete individuality; but in the mass of details the historian never forgets the central problems.

The general reader in this country knows the historical method which is termed 'prosopography' above all from the work of the late Sir Lewis Namier, whose *Parliament at the Accession of George III* appeared in 1929. It had been employed by Roman historians well before that time; Matthias Gelzer's *Die Nobilität der römischen Republik* had come out in 1912, F. Münzer's *Römische Adelsparteien und Adelsfamilien* in 1920. One may doubt, however, whether it has ever been employed more effectively than by Syme, who apart from being a great historian is a considerable literary artist. The mandarin prose of his predecessors had run to long, flowing sentences, suggesting an affinity with Isocrates or Cicero; Syme instead writes short sentences, pithy, concise, and loaded with meaning, recalling the manner of Sallust and still more of Tacitus, and echoing Gibbon. Provided one has a reasonably good memory one can read *The Roman Revolution* as though it were a memoir or a novel; anyone who enjoys St Simon need not hesitate to tackle it, and people who admire Balzac or indeed Proust will be well advised to try it.

'The political life of the Roman Republic,' Syme writes, 'was swayed, not by parties and programmes of a modern and parliamentary character, not by the ostensible opposition between Senate and People, Optimates and Populares, but by the strife for power, wealth and glory.' He calls the Roman constitution 'a screen and a sham', showing how the political dynasts used links with men of money, patronage exercised in the lawcourts and the personal allegiance of 'clients' of all kinds, ranging from freedmen to foreign monarchs, to build up their power and influence. The *nobiles*, men of consular ancestry, constituted a more or less closed circle, not easy for a 'new man' to penetrate; during the last century of the Republic they were challenged by the domination of the great generals, holders of the extraordinary commands which the growing empire had made necessary. The civil wars between the faction of Marius and Cinna and that of Sulla were followed by an uneasy interval, marked by the growing preponderance of Pompeius Magnus. Finally the main body of the *nobiles* was forced to join forces with Pompeius to resist the still more threatening power built up by Julius Caesar during his ten years as governor of Gaul. Syme's Caesar is not the superman of Mommsen, consciously planning, in the manner of Bismarck or Cavour, to put an end to the abuses of the old system by establishing a monarchy on the Hellenistic pattern. Like the brilliant German historian Hermann Strasburger, but independently of him – Strasburger's book on Caesar's entry into history came out in 1938 – Syme sees him as a typical, if exceptionally gifted, Roman aristocrat struggling with his peers for power and honours, and forced in defence of what he called his *dignitas* into the struggle with Pompeius and the Optimates whose successful conclusion carried him to supreme power.

The period of chaos, intrigue and civil strife that followed the dictator's assassination is brilliantly narrated in full detail. Syme admires the courage which Cicero showed in the last year of his life, but declines to sentimentalise him; he believes that in raising up the young Caesar 'through violence and illegal arms' against Antonius he showed himself 'fanatical and dangerous'. Marcus Antonius has had his history written largely by his enemies; Syme treats him with sympathy, pointing out that a careless and disorderly private life did not prevent him from showing on occasion 'consummate skill as a statesman', besides courage and generalship. His downfall was due partly to 'a sentiment of loyalty incompatible with the chill claims of statesmanship'. Syme does not allow the awareness of Augustus' final achievements to prevent him from describing as it happened the rise of the young adventurer, with no advantages except his status as the heir of Caesar, when he backed the *nobiles* against Antonius in the war of Mutina, seized the consulship after the opportune death in battle of both its holders, changed sides and joined Antonius in the blood-bath of the proscriptions, throwing his ally Cicero to the wolves, held on to Italy while Antonius departed for the east, avoided war before he was ready by the Pact of Brundisium and played every card correctly until the final show-down, smearing his enemy by means of a propaganda worthy of Goebbels. Syme does not depreciate the greatness of Augustus, which he says 'will the more sharply be revealed by an unfriendly presentation'. But he shows how the triumvir Octavianus, co-author of the proscriptions, turned into the defender of Rome and Italy against the oriental despotism of Antonius and Cleopatra and finally the noble and disinterested Princeps, restorer of the Republic, subtly dissociating himself from the Dictator to whose heritage he owed his start. His Antonius and his Augustus are recognisably the same as Shakespeare's.

The story is told in full detail, and with abundant wealth of documentation. Syme shows how the faction behind the young adventurer gradually expanded, incorporating more and more well-connected and respected persons, yet never lost the support of the Italian municipalities and of well-to-do supporters in the provinces, and how the Princeps gave it an ultra-respectable look by artificially reviving the relics of the ancient aristocracy by means of subsidies and honours. He describes the rise of factions within the faction, and the shifting balance of power as one plan after another for the succession to Augustus was frustrated by an adverse fortune. A thorough-going social revolution, involving the rise of a new ruling class and a change from liberty to despotism, is presented in full detail and with vivid colour; nor have subsequent discoveries or researches substantially modified the facts as here narrated.

Even if Syme can be said to have equalled this early masterpiece, he has not so far surpassed it; but it was only the first of a succession of books ranging over the whole of Roman history from the age of the Gracchi to the fall of the western empire. The flow of publication was briefly halted by the Second World War, when Syme was in Belgrade, Ankara and Constantinople. After the war, the steady stream of articles continued; in 1958 came two books, a small but significant and characteristic study called *Colonial Elites* and a masterly study of *Tacitus*, in two large volumes. The former work, dealing with Spain and the Americas as well as Rome, showed that Syme had not forgotten his New Zealand origins, which have been as useful to him as his experience in the Hampshire Militia was to Gibbon. In the *Tacitus*, the writer's command over the great body of evidence that illustrates the subject seems complete, and the history of the period is surveyed from a fresh, unprejudiced and enlightened point of view. The paradox of the historiography of the imperial period emerges clearly; the historian regretted despotism, but acknowledged its necessity, praising but not admiring the Stoic martyrs who defied it. If the book has a weakness it is that of being too sympathetic to its subject; Syme credits Tacitus with an active interest in establishing the true facts and with a freedom from contemporary prejudices not easily to be credited to a writer of his time. The same tendency may be more easily observed in a work on a far smaller scale, a lecture on Thucydides to be found in the *Proceedings of the British Academy* for 1962 (vol. 48), which makes out the historian as freer from the limits imposed by time and situation than others can imagine; here Strasburger's attitude is significantly different. Like *The Roman Revolution*, *Tacitus* is notable as a work of literary art; but the subject is less unitary and the wealth of detail even greater, so that it is less satisfying from the literary point of view. Still, it represents a quantity of learned labour that would suffice for the lifetime of a distinguished scholar; and a colleague who unlike me is an expert in the field tells me that he thinks it Syme's greatest work as a historian.

In 1964 Syme brought out a much extended version of the Sather Lectures on *Sallust* which he had given at Berkeley in 1959. By Syme's standards, this work is a little disappointing. Sallust's rhetorical moralising about the corruption of the *nobiles* is given more credit for being an effective criticism of the system than it deserves; and from being concise the style has become virtually staccato, sometimes giving, like that of Seneca, a displeasing impression of jerkiness. Yet the learning is as great as ever, and the book contains much brilliant analysis, particularly in the chapters that deal with the conspiracy of Catilina. Syme here rightly reminds us that the last age of the Republic, for all its turbulence, was 'an era of liberty, vitality and innovation'.

The last fifteen years have seen a marked renewal of interest in the problems of the late empire, and Syme has been much occupied with the difficulties posed by the series of lives of emperors attributed to six named authors that is called the *Historia Augusta*. His theory that they are the work of a single writer working at the end of the fourth century, a learned, unscrupulous and malicious writer, rather like Sir Edmund Backhouse, who reacted in a mocking spirit to the publication of the great history of Ammianus Marcellinus, has been set forth in a book (*Ammianus and the Historia Augusta*, 1968) and a whole volume of essays (*Emperors and Biography*, 1971). It has not won universal assent; but of the value of Syme's contribution to the discussion of the enigmatic work and its relevance to the history of the period there can be no doubt, and one may say the same of his penetrating remarks about ancient fiction and pseudo-history in general.

History in Ovid (1978) supplies a brilliant postscript to *The Roman Revolution*, showing the Augustan regime in its sombre last years and, while not pretending to offer a solution to a problem that is scarcely soluble, pointing in the direction in which an answer to many of the questions about the great poet's exile that one can scarcely help asking is surely to be found. Syme's findings correspond closely with those of a younger scholar in two remarkable articles that he can have seen only at a late stage of his work, one on 'Augustan poetry and the life of luxury' and another on 'Propertius and Antony', published by Jasper Griffin in the *Journal of Roman Studies* for 1976 and 1977.

But Syme is not only a writer of books; much of his best work is to be found in his numerous articles and in his occasional reviews. Some have already been collected in *Ten Studies in Tacitus* (1970), and in *Danubian Papers* (1971). Now we have a generous selection from the minor writings published between 1929 and 1970, well printed in two handsome volumes and decorated with a good photograph. The collection was originally planned to honour Sir Ronald on his seventieth birthday in 1973; its appearance was delayed in the hope that an index would be available in time, a hope that has sadly been disappointed. But we are promised an index that will embrace not only the contents of this volume but also those of the other two collections of opuscula; and we have here a bibliography of Syme's writings down to the end of 1970.

These articles range over Roman history from the second century BC until the fall of the western empire; some are especially welcome here because they were published in remote places. Historical study, like military intelligence, must construct a great framework of detail, since one can never tell whether even an apparently insignificant fact may suddenly acquire importance, and some of these articles are severely prosopographical. Syme traces missing persons and lists senators, tribes and towns with unfailing learning and acuteness; even in these technical pieces one may at any moment come upon a characteristic flash of wit or insight. But much of the book is of great general interest and importance; much of Syme's best writing can be found here. The style is recognisable even in the earliest item, the brilliant refutation of the assumption that the 'bad' emperor Domitian must have left the empire's finances in a parlous state; but as time goes on we see the sentences become shorter, the style grow more aphoristic and allusive, the idiosyncrasies more noticeable.

Some articles throw new light on famous persons – the cross-grained and independent statesman and historian Asinius Pollio, the poet, friend of Virgil and Governor of Egypt C. Cornelius Gallus, the Caesarian lieutenant and Pompeian partisan T. Labienus, Tiberius' minister and victim Sejanus, the louche Caesarian henchman – suspected of throwing live slaves to his red mullets to improve their flavour – Vedius Pollio, the famous general Corbulo (one of the seven irregularly-born children of the six-times-married Vistilia, and so half-brother of the notorious prosecutor Suillius Rufus and of Caligula's last wife). Equally revealing light is thrown upon obscure persons – upon Catullus' friend Veranius, on the possible identity of the ennobled muleteer Sabinus in the Catullan parody of the tenth poem in the *Catalepton*, on a whole group of connections of the elder Pliny, on bastards in the Roman aristocracy, and upon many more. The study of individuals yields significant general conclusions; we are shown in detail how first Italians and later provincials acquired a share in wealth and honours. Important studies are devoted to certain provinces – Pamphylia, Cilicia, Spain, Africa. There are several essays on themes of great general importance – on the reasons for the fall of the Roman Republic, on Caesar, the senate and Italy, on Livy in relation to Augustus and his regime, on the Greeks under Roman rule (this last superbly written, and illustrated with telling quotations from Bagehot and from Mr Podsnap). A brief talk on Roman historians and Renaissance politics makes one wish Syme had wandered oftener outside the confines of Roman history; it touches on Machiavelli and the Renaissance vogue for Tacitus. It contains the only real error I have discovered in the book; the school that had Camden for Head Master and Ben Jonson for a pupil was not St Paul's, but Westminster.

Like all valuable new ideas in scholarship, prosopography has been abused by minor scholars who have treated it as a key to open all doors, applying it mechanically and indiscriminately. Some such persons have even aped the master's style, some of whose idiosyncrasies lend themselves to caricature; he has been known to employ the phrase 'so far so good', employed by Widmerpool in his famous oration at the old boys' dinner at Le Bas' house. Not long ago, a gifted young Oxford historian was heard to boast that he took no interest in the study of institutions; so far have we come from the still Mommsenian Oxford that Momigliano found when he first came to England. Syme can be blamed for none of these things. He has shown Roman history from a new angle, indicated by the circumstances of his own time. Momigliano once wrote that Syme reacted directly against the exaltation of Augustus that prevailed in the 'pro-fascist circles' of the appeasers of the thirties; I would rather say that he reacted against the residual Victorian stuffiness that made people find Augustus as respectable as the Emperor Wilhelm I or Queen Victoria, and profited by the experience of being a contemporary of Hitler and Mussolini to understand such episodes as Nero's suppression of the conspiracy of Piso in a way that had not been easy for men brought up in the security of the English nineteenth century. His achievement has significantly altered our view of Roman history, and the editor of this collection is right to compare him with Barthold Georg Niebuhr and with Theodor Mommsen.

15

A Bad Press for Rome?

The historian of any empire must try to show how the imperial people got on with its subjects and with other foreigners. Some imperial peoples have been much better at this than others; without mentioning African and Asian imperialism, one may recall the record of the Germans during their short period as colonizers. Yet cruelty does not inevitably or immediately lead to disaster, or the Spaniards would have been less successful imperialists than they were. Some successful imperialists have freely intermarried with their subjects; others have strictly forbidden the practice. Kindness does not automatically beget gratitude; many Indians found English mildness, combined as it often was with mental attitudes that exasperated them, more infuriating than they would have done other people's savagery. In the case of a great empire like the Roman, involved with many foreign peoples, the phenomena are so various that generalization is not easy; we can understand only through the detailed presentation of the facts.

Dacre Balsdon was an old-fashioned Oxford tutor who put teaching first. He was also a learned and intelligent historian: and his last book, written after his retirement to a country cottage, is his best. It is extremely informative, planned and organised with great skill and written clearly, concisely and often wittily. The style is more personal and more colloquial than the usual donnish mandarin; one will find 'cissy', 'pricey', 'six of the best'. It is not only an important historical work, but an extremely entertaining book to read.

Balson begins by explaining the idea of Rome which the Romans themselves entertained, and then the special snobbery which the idea of Rome generated. This snobbery was adopted, with uncommon speed and completeness, by successive waves of new recruits to citizenship; Tacitus, a Roman consul whose family probably came from southern Gaul, finds that in a year marked by some of Tiberius's worst cruelties one of the most shocking events was the marriage of a

* A review of *Romans and Aliens* by J.P.V.D. Balsdon in the *Spectator*, October 1979.

great-granddaughter of Augustus to a rich and respectable man who, like Augustus's own grandfather, happened not to be a senator. The Romans' feelings about themselves naturally affected their attitudes to others.

By far their most important relationship with another people was what Balsdon well terms their love-hate relationship with the Greeks. Philhellenism was hardly a serious factor in Roman policy. When the Romans first became involved in Greek politics, they made much play with it; but the moment they had established their domination they threw off the mask, wiping out Corinth, letting down their principal Greek supporters, and obliterating Greek liberty. The extent of Greek support for Mithridates shows how many Greeks detested them; then Greece suffered appallingly during the civil wars, when many Greeks suported Cleopatra. Yet it would be absurd to dismiss all Roman philhellenism as a fraud. Long before their career of conquest began, the Romans had been deeply affected by the strong Greek influences they had met in Italy, something that has come to be fully understood only during this century. They created a considerable art and literature based almost entirely upon their study of Greek models; their social life and their whole culture contained a strong Greek element. Some individual Romans hated the Greeks, others greatly admired them; in general Romans esteemed their intelligence, but found them undignified and unreliable, often contrasting them unfavourably with their distinguished ancestors. Dependent though the Greeks were on Rome, they found it hard to be interested in any culture but their own: Balsdon aptly compares them with the French in this respect. Here again different individuals reacted differently to the Romans, and Balsdon displays the facts in all their complexity.

Roman feelings about 'barbarian' nations were in general simpler; westerners were brave and noble but crude and stupid, easterners were subtle and sensitive but soft and slippery. They felt most strongly about their chief rivals, the Carthaginians, whom they utterly destroyed. In Spain they annihilated Numantia; in Gaul Caesar amputated the right hands of all the defenders of Uxellodunum; in New Carthage they killed the whole population of certain parts of the town, even the animals. We are often told that the ancients knew no colour bar, but Balsdon points out that high-born Romans are not known to have intermarried with blacks, and that the Greeks and Romans thought them to feel inferior on account of their colour. Yet the speed and completeness with which Roman culture spread in Gaul, Spain and Africa is remarkable.

Next come chapters on Romans abroad, on enslavement and the buying of slaves and on the process of becoming a Roman and the

gradual extension of the citizenship. Roman generosity in granting it
had its reverse side; Balsdon points out that the Constitutio
Antoniniana of 212 AD which granted citizenship to all within the
borders of the empire gave a considerable boost to the returns from
taxes. Then follows a chapter on expulsion from one's homeland,
which tended to be a more serious matter in the ancient world than in
the modern.

The chapters on communication, the first dealing mainly with
Greek and Latin, the second with 'barbarous' languages, are of
special interest. From the second century BC educated Romans had to
know Greek; many Greeks were obliged to learn some Latin, but
they did not willingly learn foreign languages, and took no interest in
Latin literature. Writing during the second century AD Pausanias in
his guidebook tells his readers that the Latin term translated by the
familiar word 'Sebastos' is 'Augustus'. In the west Latin spread
rapidly; from the first century AD many leading Roman writers came
from Spain, Gaul and Africa. When Milton wrote that uncouth
Scotch names would have made Quintilian gasp, he forgot that
Quintilian himself came from Calagurris. At this time and for long
after cultivated people in the west learned Greek. But later in the
imperial period Greek in the west declined; Augustine was not taught
it, and Jerome and Rufinus were most unusual in having a good
knowledge of it. Latin in the east was more persistent, partly because
it was the language of law and government; in the late fourth century
the Alexandrian Greek-speaker Claudian was incomparably the best
Latin poet. Not many Romans knew 'barbarous' languages, but many
barbarians had to learn Latin, and they left their mark on it. In a
fascinating chapter about Roman names, Balsdon offers the best
discussion I know of the difficult topic of what names the Romans
at
 ^
actually called each other by in conversion.

Then in two chapters called 'A Bad Press for Rome' and 'A Good
Press for Rome' Balsdon examines the views of various persons,
including authors, who took either one line or the other. He lists many
examples of Roman rudeness, greed and tactlessness; he also lists
instances of Roman decency and tolerance. These chapters are
enlivened with amusing and intelligent sketches of some of the writers
who fall under one heading or the other. The book ends with a chapter
about different peoples known to the Romans and their looks, habits
and beliefs; here you will find sections about homosexuality, eunuchs
and circumcision, and also about magic, astrology and other
superstitions.

The book is never dull, and it contains a large assortment of
instructive and entertaining facts. Lucian describes how a noble

Roman lady, wishing to divert herself during a carriage journey with her painted boyfriend, entrusted her pet bitch to her tame Stoic philosopher, on whose lap it had puppies; the resemblance of this story to the 18th-century Milanese poem by Carlo Porta in which the priest catches his death of cold while looking after the Marchesa's lapdog underlines the likeness between the two men's positions. The word 'spurious' originated because bastards were registered as 's(ine) p(atre) f(ilius)', and with the stops and word divisions omitted this was mistaken for 'Sp. filius', SP being the common abbreviation of the Roman praenomen Spurius. The statement in the Digest that premises owned by respectable people often contained brothels will remind readers of a certain age, says Balsdon, of the matter of certain Church of England property in Paddington.

After reading the book few people will wish to sentimentalise about the Romans, but most will agree that they were a good deal better than they might have been; a Carthaginian victory in the Second Punic War would have been almost as great a disaster as a Persian conquest of Greece by Xerxes. Yet Balsdon is right to approve the remark of Fronto, Marcus Aurelius's tutor, that the Romans lacked warmth: 'they were a cold people'.

16

Women in Greece and Rome 1

The indexes of the two great social and economic histories of the Hellenistic world and of the Roman empire by Michael Ivanovitch Rostovtzeff have no entries under the heading 'Women'. There are, naturally, many books containing information about women in antiquity, and *Goddesses, Whores, Wives and Slaves* by Sarah B. Pomeroy contains a useful selection from her own extensive bibliography published in *Arethusa* for 1973. But systematic treatment of the subject has hardly been attempted; apart from two slight sketches by the German Theodor Birt (1932) and the Italian U.E. Paoli (1953), an admirable but brief paper on the equality of the sexes by Joseph Vogt in the Mainz Academy's proceedings for 1960 and J.P.V.D. Balsdon's *Roman Women* (1962; very readable, and informative about the upper reaches of society) very little can be cited. This is strange, when one considers the importance and the difficulty of some of the problems presented by the social situation of women in the ancient world.

Anyone who asks why the status of women was at no time and no place in ancient history lower than it was during the fifth century BC in Athens, supposedly the most advanced city of that age, will do so more profitably in the context of a general study of women's position in antiquity; and it is so with many other problems. In our own time, when the position of women is as much a burning topic as it has ever been, it is specially interesting to inquire into the nature of the restrictions which the societies of Greece and Rome imposed upon their female members.

The historian who attempts a serious study of this topic requires a very special training and equipment. He needs to be familiar with ancient law and with the various sources from which we know it, and with the record of transactions affecting women preserved in inscriptions and papyri. He must not only know the literary texts but must interpret them with skill and caution. The question of the value

---

* A review of *Goddesses, Whores, Wives and Slaves* by Sarah P. Pomeroy in *The Times Literary Supplement*, 26 September 1975.

of imaginative literature as a source of information about the
character and status of women is very delicate; it will not do to assume
as carelessly as many scholars have done that the depiction of Bronze
Age heroines in fifth-century tragedies is firsthand evidence for the
nature of the women known to the tragedians. He must have direct
acquaintance with a vast mass of details preserved in inscriptions, in
papyri and in works of art of many kinds; and he must know how to
select the items that are representative or significant and how to
proceed from the particular to the general, while always making full
allowance for the incompleteness of the surviving evidence. He must be
able to employ the techniques of modern anthropology and of
sociology; in particular he must know how to utilize the results of
demographic analysis, which has for some time been profitably applied
to the study of the ancient world, without ever forgetting that in most
instances both the nature and the extent of the evidence available
enjoin the greatest caution.

Professor Pomeroy fulfils every one of these requirements. She was a
pupil of the papyrologist of Columbia University, John Day, who was
himself a pupil of Rostovtzeff, and she is admirably equipped for the
strenuous task which she has chosen. A study of the topic from the
Bronze Age to Constantine is in some ways even harder to produce if it is
on this scale than it would be if it were in several volumes. But Professor
Pomeroy contrives to offer a great quantity of detailed information, and
the book is so well organised and the balance between the different
topics so skilfully maintained, that every item has its proper place
within the whole. She is fully conscious of the complexity of the subject,
and never over-simplifies; but she has a gift for concise and trenchant
generalisation on the right occasion. The work is written with a
scholarly detachment far removed from any partisan approach; but
Professor Pomeroy's standpoint is clearly that of a reasoned and
enlightened sympathy with women's aspirations. Scholars will find the
book indispensable, and any general reader interested in the topic will
find it both instructive and enjoyable. The need for a full-length study
remains, and Professor Pomeroy is obviously the person who should
undertake it; but the existence of this book renders that need
appreciably less urgent.

Professor Pomeroy begins by arguing that the subordination of
Greek women is reflected in the nature of the Olympian pantheon.
Men, she thinks, fearing the fully realised female, personified different
female attributes in different goddesses. The fact that modern women
are frustrated by being forced to choose between being an Athena – an
intellectual, asexual career woman – or an Aphrodite – a frivolous sex
object – or a respectable wife and mother like Hera shows that the

Greek goddesses continue to be archetypes of female existence. 'If the characteristics of the major goddesses were combined', she writes, 'a whole being with unlimited potential for development – a female equivalent of Zeus or Apollo – would emerge.' She considers theories about a primitive earth religion centring on goddesses and supposed to have been displaced by the religion of Zeus and his siblings and offspring and about an early period of matriarchy, but prudently recognises that the evidence for their existence is insufficient. Inspiration comes to heroes, she remarks, chiefly from the virgin goddesses; she approves of the idea that 'these men could feel secure only with a virgin'.

But Hera was the patroness of Jason, and doubtless favoured Argive heroes in the Theban epic as she does in the *Iliad*; etymology suggests that in the early stages of the myth she was the friend, and not the enemy, of Heracles. Her ability to hold her own in domestic conflict might be held to indicate that in early times not all Greek wives were helpless victims.

Professor Pomeroy finds that the early Greek epic shows little trace of 'the misogyny that taints later Greek literature'; she admirably describes the great female characters of Homer. Were women prized because so few were reared, and because they were useful when it came to gift-exchanges? At any rate, they had a status at this time which they seem to have lost later; but one must remember that most of the women described by Homer came from the upper reaches of society. Professor Pomeroy is always aware of the existence of social and economic differences, and rightly protests against the habit of lumping all women together without keeping these in mind.

Archaeological evidence seems to Professor Pomeroy to indicate that 'sex roles that will be familiar to the modern reader were firmly established in the Dark Age in Athens'. Women were closely associated with the rituals that concerned the dead, and the small material available indicates that they had less expectation of life than men, a conclusion not inconsistent with the demographic patterns found in later preindustrial societies. During the Archaic Age women in western Greece already enjoyed more privileges than women in the east, as the institutions of Sparta and of Gortyn in Crete – the Gortyn code was inscribed during the fifth century, but must largely reflect conditions that originated earlier – serve to indicate. The Spartans realised that the mothers of their future warriors were important to the state, and allowed their women to take physical exercise and to enjoy a modicum of freedom. The Ionian Greeks, who had orientals as near neighbours, treated their women not so very differently from orientals.

Pederasty, however, was commoner and aroused less disapproval in western than in eastern Greece. Did the comparative familiarity of the Spartan women breed some contempt? The Athenian democracy, of all Greek communities the most repressive towards women, was also the most intolerant of male homosexuality. Did the Athenian democrats guard their women closely because they prized them, at any rate as sex objects?

Professor Pomeroy gives, in her fourth chapter, an excellent account of the modern discussion of the treatment of women in fifth-century Athens; she does not quote Burckhardt, but her conclusions resemble his. While rejecting the extreme view that the life of an Athenian woman at this time was little better than that of a slave in a harem, she firmly resists the attempt of the late A.W. Gomme, in an article published fifty years ago,[1] to show that 'there is no reason to suppose that in the matter of the consequence and social freedom of women Athens was different from other Greek cities, or the classical from the Homeric age', Gomme relied too heavily on the assumption that the heroines of classic tragedy were modelled directly on contemporary women, and paid little attention to the evidence of the Attic orators.

Professor Pomeroy, on the other hand, starts by examining the laws and institutions concerning marriage and showing how women were treated as instruments for the preservation of family property; though women often transmitted this, no women ever really owned it. Pericles's law of 451-450 BC forbidding marriage with a foreigner – relaxed under the strain imposed by the Peloponnesian War, but re-enacted towards the end of the fifth century – shows how marriage was employed in the service of the closed corporation of Athenian citizens. Citizen women were denied a proper education; many of them married as early as fourteen; Pericles himself said that the most reputable one was the one who was least talked about. The picture of domestic life obtained from the orators, from comedy – if we make proper allowance for its element of fantasy – and from the dialogues of Plato fits with Professor Pomeroy's conclusion that in comparison with archaic Athens classical Athens forced its women into obscurity.

The most independent women tended to be aristocrats; and the curbing of aristocratic privilege by the democracy entailed, as Professor Pomeroy points out, the repression not only of these but of all women. In a characteristically terse paragraph she suggests that after all other forms of superiority had been eliminated the Athenian demos had to have other groups to which it could feel superior, and

[1] 'The position of women in Athens in the fifth and fourth centuries BC', in *Essays in Greek History and Literature* (1937) (first published in *CP* 20 (1925)).

picked on foreigners, slaves and women for that purpose.

Professor Pomeroy rightly warns against overestimating the value of tragedy as firsthand evidence for the character of fifth-century women. Tragedies, of course, were not written by or about common men; if their characters reflect contemporary life, it is the life of the elite which they reflect. She points out that in several tragedies, such as the plays of the *Oresteia* and the *Antigone*, the theme of·a conflict between male and female indicates that the question of women's rights was in the air, just as the *Ecclesiazusae* of Aristophanes shows that advanced theories about the position of women very like those afterwards put forward by Plato must have been current at about the end of the fifth century. While having no truck either with those who have thought Euripides to be a feminist or with those who have thought him a misogynist, Professor Pomeroy shows how much interesting matter about women and their lives his plays contain.

In the section 'Utopian Literature' Professor Pomeroy rightly remarks that Plato's critique of marriage and the family foreshadows the ideas of radical feminists of later times. Plato saw no basic difference, other than the biological, between the sexes, and was prepared to allow women exercise and education and to admit some of them to the dominant class of Guardians in his *Republic*. Yet, though he thought some women superior to some men, he thought men on the whole superior to women; and, in the less utopian prescriptions of the *Laws*, he tried to reinforce the traditional roles of both sexes, so as to make girls gentle and boys aggressive. Feminists who are disposed to idealise Plato for his championship of women should note that in the *Laws* a man who has offended against his parents may be whipped so long as he is under thirty, but that a woman guilty of the same crime may be whipped so long as she is under forty.

Even from the earliest times the women of the upper classes had been more independent than the rest, and the tendency became more evident than ever during the Hellenistic age, when numerous Greek royal dynasties came into being. In fifth-century Athenian society, as Burckhardt, referring to Plato's *Symposium*, pointed out, women made no contribution to the tone of social life; that could not be true of a society that contained among its dominating figures magnificent princesses like Arsinoe Philadelphos or Cleopatra VII. At lower social levels also, epigraphic evidence attests the growing importance of women in public life. Some of them were very rich, not only in the new kingdoms but in ancient communities like that of Sparta. In Egypt, the part of the Hellenistic world we are best informed about, Greek women still needed a guardian when acting in legal and financial matters, but their rights were more extensive than in fifth-century communities, and it seems likely that in many cases the guardianship was a matter of form. Stoic and neo-Pythagorean philosophers might take a conservative view of women's rights and duties, but Epicurus and the Cynics were more indulgent, and in this expressed the tendency of the time.

Professor Pomeroy is rightly cautious about using the evidence of the Athenian New Comedy, with its wish-fulfilment plots; but it certainly indicates that in late fourth-century Athens, even when Demetrius of Phalerum was curbing female extravagances, many citizens loved and respected their wives, and many wives, especially rich wives, nagged their husbands. Women of the lower classes were naturally less emancipated; but even these improved their position during the Hellenistic period.

The social changes of that age combined with Roman elements, Professor Pomeroy remarks, to produce the emancipated but respected upper-class woman of the late Roman republic and the empire. She shows how the position of Roman women, at first circumscribed by the customs of a patriarchal society that placed them firmly under parental or marital control, and subject to old-fashioned restrictions even as late as the third century BC, came in the end to be a good deal more enviable than it had been in any Greek society. The existence of an alternative form of marriage which left the wife a member of her father's family instead of passing into that of her husband facilitated female emancipation.

The social reforms of Augustus were in the long run powerless against the movement of the times; and the freedom that during the last century of the republic had found its extremest expression in the actions of noble ladies like Sempronia, the friend of Catiline, Fulvia, the wife of Antony, or that Clodia who may or may not have been Lesbia continued without a break into the imperial period. Many women were not only rich but highly educated; many had great influence in public life; so many examples come to hand that Servilia, Brutus's mother and Caesar's mistress, and the younger Antonia, during Tiberius's seclusion on Capri the most socially important person in Rome, do not find a mention here. A good chapter on the women of the lower classes makes full use of recent studies of the lives of slaves and freedmen. The last chapter sketches the place of women in the religion of the Romans; as the state cults declined, oriental superstitions became more popular.

In the brief epilogue Professor Pomeroy remarks that all through antiquity men seem to have been more numerous than women; female infanticide continued to be practised, and seems to have been commoner in Hellenistic than in classical times. Greece and Rome, she reminds us, were warrior societies, and what mattered above all else was victory in war.

Further, Greek society in the not too distant past had been based upon kinship groups regulated by taboos lineally descended from those of the primitive groups whose males hunted while their females prepared food. It is not surprising that Greek society was repressive towards women, or that even as late as the fourth century the patronising attitude of Aristotle was more representative than the radical attitude of Plato. Yet Professor Pomeroy reminds us that the Greeks were the first people, so far as we know, among whom the subordinate role assigned to women was called in question. She has shown how the improved status of women of the Hellenistic age contributed to their further emancipation during the late Roman republic and the early empire. Throughout antiquity many women's lives must have been miserable, and this applies especially to the vast multitudes who lived in obscurity; yet the number that attained some degree of happiness seems to have increased in Roman times, partly through the deepening of the marital relationship and the decline of homosexual inclinations.

17

Women in Greece and Rome 2

Hunting the other day through one of the vast cooperative paperback bookstores, on which the modern American university so disastrously depends, for the section devoted to the ancient classics, I found it uncomfortably hemmed in between 'Black Studies', 'Gay Studies' and 'Women's Studies'. My distress was mitigated by the discovery that the 'Women's Studies' section contained a large pile of copies of Sarah Pomeroy's learned and judicious account of women in the ancient world, *Goddesses, Whores, Wives and Slaves*.

Mary R. Lefkowitz and Maureen Fant's *Women in Greece and Rome* is another reminder that even a work dealing with a fashionable topic may be useful. 'It is intended' in the words of its compilers, 'to make accessible to people who do not know the ancient languages the kind of material on which histories of women in the ancient world must base their work.' Its unpleasing physical appearance and the presence of a certain number of misprints and errors detract little from its value.

No two scholars would make quite the same selection from the large body of available material, but this is an excellent selection, and will satisfy most readers. Literary texts are valuably supplemented by the evidence of inscriptions and papyri. Legal documents are used effectively to show women's position as it was determined by the law. Medical literature is impressively, but perhaps rather too extensively, made use of. It shows how much help women in antiquity might expect against specifically feminine complaints, and one gathers that by modern standards this appears deficient. Much material is assembled from various sources to illustrate the daily life of women. The six pages of notes are in general admirable (though I must except note 4, with its odd suggestions about sexual implications in Alcman's Louvre Partheneion) and one regrets that there are not more of them.

* A review of *Women in Greece and Rome* edited by Mary R. Lefkowitz and Maureen Fant in *The Times Literary Supplement*, 1 September 1978. (A revised and expanded version of this book will soon appear from Duckworth.)

Some of the texts are translated by the editors themselves; others are reproduced from other books, which books one must go to the preface to discover. In view of their purpose the editors rightly prefer literal renderings. Most of these are adequate, particularly those by the editors themselves, but a number seem a trifle flat. The editors rightly include the wonderful description of an encounter with a girl in the recently discovered Cologne fragment of an epode of Archilochus, since some of those who have made asses of themselves by disputing its authenticity have gone so far as to argue that no man ever talked to an unmarried woman in private before the Hellenistic age; but they have taken over a feeble rendering by John Van Sickle, which they themselves could certainly have improved on.

The strain of misogynism in Greek poetry apparent early on in Hesiod and Semonides and still being worked by the mimographers of the Hellenistic age, should not encourage one to claim that Greek women were systematically ground down by a male chauvinist tyranny; but their place in Greek society, as in every archaic society of which we have knowledge, was subordinate. Attic law treated a woman as a mere mechanism for generating children and transmitting property. How much a woman lay in the power of her husband is seen in the first oration of Lysias, whose speaker vividly describes how he caught his wife in adultery and exercised his legal right to kill her lover. His tone expresses a repulsive self-satisfaction, and the same impression is conveyed, though in a different degree, by the insufferably smug lecture of Ischomachus on how a husband ought to train his wife, in Xenophon's treatise on household management. In Menander's *Disagreeable Man*, the heroine is said to be the ideal bride; however, she has been brought up in the country, with no female relatives to teach her bad habits, by a stern father who beats her. Aristotle's view of woman's place in society is representative of his time: 'The slave', he writes, 'has no deliberative faculty at all; the woman has, but it is without authority.' Uneducated as they were, women were often superstitious. Spartan women were freer than those of Athens, probably because the mothers of future soldiers had to live a healthy life; we get exquisite glimpses of Spartan girls in Alcman, and in the last chorus of Aristophanes' *Lysistrata*.

Of course, innumerable women were loved and respected by their menfolk; this is clear from the praises of them that are quoted, condescending though some of these may sound. Epic and dramatic texts are not cited in this book; but it is not safe to deny that the portrayal of legendary heroines in literature – like the prevalent worship of goddesses – tells us nothing about the ancient attitude to femininity. In the upper reaches of society women clearly had more scope for exercising their special gifts, though evidence is sadly lacking. One did not have to be a *hetaira*, like Pericles' mistress Aspasia, to achieve this. Cimon's sister Elpinice was equally distinguished; a potsherd used for voting in an ostracism bears the legend, 'Let Cimon go, and take Elpinice with him'. During the Hellenistic age, when much of the Greek world was ruled by monarchies, notable princesses made their appearance, from Arsinoe and Berenice in the third century BC to Cleopatra in the first.

More significantly still, Greek society was the first in which doubts about the justice of women's subordination were expressed. Such doubts were found in the mouths of characters in fifth century drama, surely reflecting the theories of contemporary sophists; these and the parodies of comedy indicate that Plato was not the first to contend that women differed only biologically from men, and should have the same kind of physical and mental training.

The woman as artist was the exception rather than the rule. We hear of women painters, but time has not spared their works. The chief women poets of the early period – Sappho in the sixth century, Corinna, whom I would place in the fifth, and Erinna, perhaps writing in the fourth – seem to have written principally for an audience of women, which may indicate that in some communities women had a social life, as they had certain religious observances, in which men did not share. The society Sappho lived in is a mystery to us, though it was evidently affected by its nearness to the Oriental civilisation of Lydia. The belief that Sappho presided over a kind of educational establishment, held by Wilamowitz but derided by Sir Denys Page, is now shown by a papyrus[1] to have been shared by at least one ancient scholar; since he had access to the poet's complete works, which we have not, we ought now to hesitate to rule it out. Sappho is supreme among women poets; but Erinna's elegy for a much-loved friend who died in childbirth, though extant only in mutilated scraps, has a note of authentic passion. Otherwise, Greek women's poetry does not amount to much; there are some competent Hellenistic epigrammatists and some indifferent versifiers of the imperial period.

The early Romans were markedly repressive of their women; as late as the second century BC, Cato the Censor could clearly count on a large measure of support in maintaining the traditional attitude. Yet stories of republican heroines indicate that on occasion they might show the indomitable Roman spirit even in opposition to males; and when the now rich and powerful Roman aristocracy came into close

---

[1] See Page, *Supplementum Lyricis Graecis*, 1974, S261A (p. 25).

contact with Greek civilization, its women developed many of the characteristics of the great ladies of the Hellenistic age. In theory, Roman women were totally subordinate to their fathers or their husbands; in practice, women like the beautiful, witty and depraved Catilinarian conspirator Sempronia, the Servilia who was mistress of Caesar and mother of Brutus, and that Clodia who, whether or not she knew Catullus, provided Cicero with material for a superb tirade against her extravagances, showed plenty of independence. During the imperial period the tendency continued; the Catonian tradition could always provide a norm against which moralising rhetoricians might measure the degeneracy of the present, yet one sees how much Juvenal enjoys what he pretends horrifies him. Of course many women upheld the standards of republican virtue; the Stoic martyrs of resistance had wives as stoical as themselves, and the younger Pliny's wife, Calpurnia Hispulla, went so far as to learn her husband's works by heart and to set to music and sing his probably appalling verses.

In poetry, Roman women scarcely got off the ground. The only Roman woman poet in this book is Sulpicia, an aristocratic lady of the time of Augustus; the tone of her amatory elegies is frank, but not coarse, as the translation printed in this book makes it.

The spread of Christianity owed much to women; yet St Paul's attitude towards them conserves a strong element of traditionalist misogyny, evidently accentuated by feelings of guilt engendered by repression. The book includes moving accounts of the endurance under persecution shown by certain early Christian female martyrs; Mrs Lefkowitz has already in an article[2] made the interesting suggestion that the obstinate adherence to the Church shown by Perpetua was partly motivated by a desire to escape the repressive domination of the male members of her family.

[2] *Journal of the American Academy of Religion* 44/3 (1976) 417f.

18

Greek Homosexuality

Many scholars have been or are preoccupied with the similarities between the ancient and the modern world, and some tend to find such similarities even where they do not exist. In the past scholars have done this chiefly because for them the history of the ancient world presents a continuous development culminating in Christianity, or in modern liberalism; but now many look for likenesses in a pathetic attempt to curry favour with their modern readers by making out antiquity to have been more like our own times than it actually was.

Nowadays the best scholars are usually more concerned with the differences between then and now; and Sir Kenneth Dover is one of the best classical scholars now living. He is a very learned man indeed; 25 years ago Arnaldo Momigliano remarked to me that Dover already knew more about the fifth century BC in Greece than any man living, and he has not been idle since that time. Even more impressive than his learning is his power of seeing objectively what the ancient data tell us without reading modern notions into what he finds there. Three years ago he brought out a remarkable book called *Greek Popular Morality*, based on the excellent observation that the best way of studying the subject was to examine the moral notions taken for granted in their appeals to juries by the authors of the 150 or so Athenian political and forensic speeches of the fifth and fourth centuries that survive. Not surprisingly, this work has received the honour of an unfavourable notice from Arthur W.H. Adkins, who, having preached in his doctoral thesis the gospel that Greek ethics are deficient by the standards of modern provincial nonconformity, has repeated it in a series of writings that supply a staple protein for *bienpensant* readers. Dover's new book valuably supplements his study of Greek popular ethics by helping to extend the picture of the Greek cultural pattern which the earlier work presents. All the Greek is

---

* A review of *Greek Homosexuality* by K.J. Dover in the *New Statesman*, 6 October 1978.

translated, and the book can easily be read by non-specialists; it is a work of consummate scholarship, and no professional student of the Greeks can afford to miss it. At the same time it is a contribution to the understanding of human society that deserves to be studied well beyond professional circles.

In the past, scholars have touched with impatience and dispatched with reluctance the subject of the book. Wilamowitz was no prude; yet he seldom mentions the obvious truth that in ancient Greece young men inspired men with far deeper erotic emotions than women did, and when Pierre Louys in a novel presented Sappho as a Lesbian, he sprang to the defence of 'a pure wife and mother'. Even Burckhardt in his history of Greek culture shies off the subject. In England, Jowett translated the episode of Plato's *Symposium* in which Alcibiades tries to vamp Socrates in such a way that it is hard for the reader to see what is really happening. The aesthetes of the *fin de siècle* found the topic fascinating, but were unable to discuss it without introducing overtones of decadence more relevant to the age of Hadrian and his Antinous than to archaic and classical Greece. Now the subject can be discussed objectively, and we must be thankful, but without too much self-congratulation; there are topics – slavery, for instance – which are now harder to discuss rationally than they were half a century ago. It is of the greatest interest, for without an honest assessment of this factor the cultural pattern of ancient Greece cannot be properly understood. The problem of the status of women is linked with it; and so is the part played by love in the philosophy of Plato. Also, by examining the attitudes to sexual questions of communities remote in time and place from our own, we may make it easier for ourselves to consider them with a mind free from bias.

Dover warns us at the start that the evidence bearing on ancient homosexuality is of very different kinds, and that when we assess it we must allow for the differences in question. As in the case of Greek popular morality, the evidence of the law-courts is especially valuable; and here we are fortunate in possessing a speech in which the fourth-century politician Aeschines prosecuted Timarchus, an adherent of his enemy Demosthenes, for violation of the law forbidding those who had been male prostitutes to engage in civic life. The core of the book is a detailed study of that speech and its implications; Dover surveys in turn the different questions which the speech raises, illustrating each not only from the speech itself but from the whole body of relevant evidence. Later he deals with special aspects and developments of the subject, such as the exploitation of homosexuality in comedy and in philosophy, the homosexuality of women, and finally homosexuality in myth and history.

Much of the evidence comes from art, particularly from painted vases; and Dover has examined this with great thoroughness. He gives an excellent selection of illustrations, all the more welcome because museums are often unwilling to exhibit and scholars to reproduce the works of art most relevant to his purpose, some of which are not only interesting but delightful. In his text he gives a detailed account of the sexual tastes and tendencies revealed by this material, together with the literary evidence; he thinks the supremacy of homosexual love in the Greek imagination is clearly brought out by the pronounced interest, both theoretical and practical, in the female buttocks which the evidence reveals.

The speech against Timarchus indicates, and the remainder of the evidence confirms, that homosexuality as such was not generally disapproved of. The prosecutor openly avows that he has been in love with various young men, and has been involved in quarrels because of it. Such conduct was thought perfectly normal, but young men who allowed their lovers sexual favours were disapproved of; Dover aptly compares the way in which modern societies tolerate men who pursue women but condemn those women who grant them sexual favours.

This conclusion is confirmed by evidence from early lyric and elegiac poetry, which often celebrates homosexual love; from comedy, which exploits the subject for the purposes of humour; from Plato's picture of the society moved in by Socrates, and by his use of love for beautiful persons as a stage on the way towards a love for beautiful ideas. Dover shows great finesse in using each kind of evidence just as its nature warrants and no further, and the book is full of acute treatments of subsidiary problems.

Dover observes that Homer makes no overt allusion to homosexuality, though he knows the myth of Ganymede; he does not give the friendship of Achilles and Patroclus the erotic colouring which it certainly had in the trilogy which Aeschylus devoted to the subject. I wonder if he suspects, as I do, that Aeschines was right in interpreting Homer's silence as 'a sign of cultivated sensitivity'. This would be by no means the only instance of deliberate avoidance by the epic poets of topics which they felt inappropriate to epic poetry; and as Dover says, the rate of change of Greek attitudes, practices and institutions was very slow. The prevalence of homosexuality in archaic and classical times cannot have been a sudden development following upon universal heterosexuality during the epic age, any more than the prevalence of a belief in ritual pollution. Dover gives sound reasons for rejecting the belief that homosexuality was specifically Dorian and entered Greece with the Dorian invaders. He finds its origins in a contempt for women that arose in early times when the community depended entirely on the valour of the warrior; perhaps it goes back to the primitive age when the males belonging to the hunting group were often separated from their women and their children.

Dover points out the vast difference between the Greek attitude towards homosexuality and that of a culture which has inherited a prohibition against it originally supposed to rest upon divine authority, with the result that conservative persons tend to recoil from it in horror and persons who fancy themselves to be rebels tend to approve of it, even if they feel no wish to practise it. He warns us that the modern tendency to consider the world as divided into homosexuals and heterosexuals is a local accident; Proust would have agreed with him. There were in ancient Greece, as there are today, many people who markedly preferred homosexual to heterosexual activity; there were also many who had the opposite preference to a marked degree; but there were also many people, perhaps a majority, who enjoyed both and if given an opportunity would indulge in either. 'Confronted by cultures older and richer and more elaborate than theirs,' Dover writes, 'cultures which none the less differed greatly from each other, the Greeks felt free to select, adapt, develop, and – above all – innovate. Fragmented as they were into tiny political units, they were constantly aware of the extent to which morals and manners are local.'

19

Classical Attitudes to Modern Issues

Mr Wilkinson is known as the author of attractively written books about Augustan poetry and of a good general summary of the Roman achievement. It is fitting that in a series of lectures given in memory of Lord Northcliffe he should enlighten the general public about the classical attitudes to such fashionable modern issues as 'Population and Family Planning', 'Women's Liberation', 'Nudism in Deed and Word' (nudism in word turns out to be what is usually called obscenity) and 'Homosexuality'.

Though in his introduction the author expresses gratitude to two living English scholars, the small book has no room for learned references. It is based for the most part on literary texts, and shields its readers from direct acquaintance with the non-literary texts which a full study of these subjects has to use. It happens that the topics dealt with here have lately formed the subject of scholarly works which go into them more searchingly than could be done in narrow space, and which are perfectly accessible to the general reader. For the subject-matter of the first two chapters we may consult a general study in Sarah Pomeroy's *Goddesses, Whores, Wives and Slaves* and a collection of source material in translation in *Women in Greece and Rome*, by Mary Lefkowitz and Maureen Fant.[1] These authors make extensive use of the great body of material found in papyri and inscriptions and in medical and other technical literature. Homosexuality together with obscenity is admirably dealt with in Sir Kenneth Dover's *Greek Homosexuality*.[2] At a scientific level Mr Wilkinson does not pretend to compete with works of this kind. Most of his material is drawn from literary texts; on occasion he uses a little too trustingly the anecdotage in which ancient literary texts abound. But his book has many virtues; it is clearly and attractively written, and contains much sound sense.

Questions of population in the ancient world are notoriously difficult, and Mr Wilkinson leaves aside 'the vexed question of figures'

* A review of *Classical Attitudes to Modern Issues* by L.P. Wilkinson in the *Spectator*, 16 June 1979.

[1] See above, ch.16. [2] See above, ch.18.

and concentrates on attitudes. A central fact emerging from his work is that in all these matters the ancients were unencumbered with religious dogmas. In early times the birthrate was too high, since Greece is a poor country and not more than 14 per cent of its soil is arable; hence the Greeks exposed many infants and planted many colonies abroad. In early times brides had to be paid for, since few females were reared; later, fathers had to pay bridegrooms to take their daughters off their hands. The Romans, on the other hand, had plenty of space and needed soldiers; under the empire, when the birthrate began to fall, the government took measures to keep it up. Neither when the birthrate was too high nor when it was too low did religious considerations prevent people from considering the matter objectively. Methods of contraception and abortion were primitive, but they could be applied without interference based on dogmatic grounds. The ancients were also free from the sentimental belief in the sanctity of human life that leads so many moderns to preserve and cosset imbeciles and monsters.

The world of ancient Greece, especially in the archaic and classical periods, was a man's world. Mrs Pomeroy has remarked that Athens, in so many respects the most enlightened of the Greek communities, was in this respect one of the most reactionary; in Sparta, where women were valued as potential mothers of fighting men, they had greater freedom. During the Hellenistic and Roman periods their position improved somewhat, at least in the higher reaches of society. Yet it is remarkable that the great dramatists of the fifth century show themselves aware of the problems raised by the subjection of women and make effective use of the tensions that may arise as a result of them; before the end of the century, philosophers had begun the objective discussion of these questions. So far as we know this happened in no other western communities before comparatively recent times.

The early Greeks differed markedly from Asiatics in their attitude to nakedness; nothing like the nudity of Greek athletes or the nudity observable in Greek art could be found among the neighbours of the Greeks. This had nothing to do with sexual licence, any more than it does in modern Japan, where mixed bathing in the nude is permitted but it is thought rude to inspect one's fellow bathers; the nudity of hetairas at dinner-parties was a different matter. People went naked at the right place and time; just so, obscenity was allowed at some times and places, but not at others. Comedy and other literary genres allowed obscenity, which was probably a survival of the obscenity permitted during certain religious rites and meant originally to encourage fertility; in other literary genres, such as epic, lyric and tragedy, obscenity was carefully avoided. The objections to it were grounded not on dogmas about sin, but on good taste and hygiene.

Mr Wilkinson acknowledges a debt to an article on homosexuality which Dover published in 1964, and deals with the question very much along the lines Dover has followed in the book he published last year. In Athens lovers were not blamed for pursuing their loved ones, but the loved ones were blamed if they gave in, as in modern times young men are not blamed if they pursue girls but girls are blamed if they let themselves be caught; in the military aristocracies of Crete and Sparta, homosexuality was institutionalised. Many people in antiquity disapproved of it, some of them, like Plato, on the ground that it was unnatural; but we find nothing like the horror of it which was inspired by Christianity. It was common for the same person to indulge both in homosexual and heterosexual practices, although some had a distinct preference for the one or for the other; the modern neurotic homosexual whose relations with his mother have gone wrong is a type seldom to be identified in ancient literature.

One of the best reasons for studying classical antiquity is that it helps us to avoid insularity in space and time; we learn that some beliefs which we have never dreamed of questioning did not always remain unquestioned, and vice versa. This book shows how certain attitudes which till lately seemed highly shocking to most members of our own society, but which now no longer do so, were not uncommon in the ancient world. This is refreshing; and it allows us both to congratulate our own society on being so enlightened and to encourage it to pat the ancients on the head for having anticipated its enlightenment. It is sometimes just as interesting, though less conducive to popularity, to note cases in which the ancients did not share opinions that now form part of bien-pensant orthodoxy, such as the view that not the criminal but society is to blame for crime or the view that the uncivilised will somehow become civilised if they are given power over those who are civilised.

20

The Olympic Games

In an Olympic year many people will feel curious about the history of the Olympic Games, modern and ancient. There is an obvious demand for a handsome illustrated volume, edited by no less a person than Lord Killanin, the Chairman of the International Olympic Committee, with the collaboration of an experienced journalist, in which many well-qualified contributors cover various aspects of the subject. Separate treatment is given to each of the Olympic sports; there are full lists of winners and of records; and each celebration of the Games since their revival in 1896 is given a section to itself, written, where this is possible, by an eye-witness. Some parts of the books will be of interest even to people not devoted to sport, but by far the least satisfactory section of the book is that devoted to the Olympic Games of the ancient world. Innocently supposing that a Greek must be the best person to write about Greek history, the editors have consigned the topic to the retired Director of the Greek National Academy of Physical Education, who swamps the reader in a mass of trivial details. But by great good luck there appears simultaneously an account of the ancient games which few living writers could improve on. Anything by Professor Finley is learned, intelligent and good to read; and his Dutch collaborator, Professor Pleket, is especially familiar with the epigraphic evidence on which much of our knowledge of the ancient games depends. A book which tells us that Roman Hercules is the same as Greek Heracles and that Augustus was the first Roman emperor cannot be accused of being too esoteric to obtain a wide circulation in an Olympic year.

The Greeks could not remember a time when they had no athletic contests; their early epics mention funeral games in honour of dead heroes. In legend the Olympic Games had Heracles for founder, and in practice we can follow their history from the eighth century before

---

* A review of *The Olympic Games: 80 Years of People, Events and Records* edited by Lord Killanin and John Rodda, and of *The Olympic Games: The First Thousand Years* by M.I. Finley and H.W. Pleket in the *Spectator*, 14 February 1976.

Christ: only during the fourth century AD did the triumph of Christianity lead to their suppression. No other race or nation of the ancient world had any comparable institution; and the Greek love of athletics is all the more notable when one remembers that they had no lack of wars. That intense competitiveness in which Burckhardt saw one of their distinguishing features was not shared by any of their neighbours. Something very like it reappeared at the time of the revival of an interest in the ancient culture; and during the nineteenth century, when modern Europe made its most systematic attempt to enter into the cultural inheritance of ancient Greece, it once more manifested itself through organised athletics.

Both the books give interesting information about Baron Pierre de Coubertin, the founder of the modern Olympic Games. He was stimulated by the wish to remedy a neglect of physical education in France which he thought had contributed to the defeat by Prussia; but it was not only for his own country, nor for his own class, that Coubertin wished to secure the benefits of organised athletic competition. He was a convinced internationalist, strongly opposed to the chauvinism of his times; and though he believed in an élite, he believed in an élite of excellence and not of birth or wealth. Physical excellence seemed to him closely linked with mental excellence, and he wished the amateurs who competed in the Games to be animated by a lofty conception of fair play and international amity. Coubertin had to struggle against every kind of opposition. He had many enemies in his own country, where chauvinism was by no means weak; and he had to work hard to persuade the representatives of the nations to sink their differences and work together for what he saw as the common good. When he arranged for the first modern games to be held in Athens, the Greek government first opposed the project and later, when it had proved a great success, tried to take over the Olympic movement; soon after, an American group made a similar attempt. The First World War seemed to ruin all Coubertin's hopes, but he persisted, and the Games were held in Antwerp in 1920, with complete success.

Like other forms of idealism, Olympic idealism nourishes its own kind of absurdities. Henri Pouret in an article on 'Art and the Olympics' claims that each Olympic event is a powerful inspiration for the arts. 'This makes it possible,' he continues, 'to say that Olympism, consisting of a spiritualisation of muscular movement, leads sport to become one with thought, creating, or rather discovering, Platonic humanism ...' The Russian weight-lifter Vassily Alexeev, whose photograph appears in the book, certainly looks as if his thought has become one with sport. In 1912 an 'Ode to Sport', written in German and purporting to be by Martin Essbach and Georg Hohrod, was entered for the Olympic poetry competition. It was actually a translation from the French of Coubertin, who did not wish his poem to be given special favour; but despite his action it obtained a gold medal.

What are the main differences between ancient and modern Olympism? As a tough-minded realist, Professor Finley is always on guard against the tendency to idealise the ancient world, and he points out that the ancient notion of amateurism did not quite coincide with that of Coubertin. It is true, as Ruskin noted, that the official Olympic prize was nothing more valuable than a crown of wild olive; but as early as the fifth century BC and for long after that, athletes, even if they were aristocrats, expected and obtained material rewards. Even in antiquity, civic communities thought their prestige enhanced by the victories of their athletes; nor did the competitors subscribe to Coubertin's ideal of sportsmanship. Chivalry towards defeated opponents is no part of the attitude even of the great lyric poet, Pindar, who during the fifth century BC wrote many odes in praise of victors in the games. The theory that what mattered most was not to win but to compete seems to have been first put forward by a Bishop of Pennsylvania in a sermon preached in 1908; what the Greeks cared about was victory. Yet the ancient Games had some advantages over the modern.

First, the ancient Games were strictly a Greek institution. Even the Macedonians had difficulty, as late as the fifth century BC, in establishing their title to compete, and though eventually the Romans had to be granted privileged status, 'barbarians' were not admitted. There was general agreement about the rules and about the essential nature of the competition, which like the other great games of Greece formed part of a religious festival. The Games were administered by the citizens of the tiny city-state of Elis, whose very insignificance made it far easier for their authority to be accepted than it would have been if one of the great powers, say Sparta or Athens, had controlled the festival. And on the whole, war and politics were prevented from spoiling the Olympic atmosphere.

In contrast, the modern Olympics are open to all nations; and grave problems result from this aspiration. Before Hitler came to power, the International Olympic Committee had innocently assigned the 1936 Olympics to Berlin. In 1935 Hitler decreed that Jews and Blacks were sub-human; Ernest Lee Jahncke, the American representative on the IOC, opposed his country's participation and was expelled. When the President of the IOC paid a preliminary visit to the venue of the Winter Games, he found that the lavatories bore the notice 'Dogs and

Jews Not Allowed', and had to argue with Hitler before they were removed. Luckily the star of the Games, and of the famous film Leni Riefenstahl made of them, proved to be a Black American, Jesse Owens.

Such problems have not ceased to trouble the Olympic movement. First South Africa, then Rhodesia was expelled; Communist China competed in 1952, but withdrew later, when a representative of Chiang Kai-shek's regime was elected to the IOC. Much trouble has been caused by differences of outlook, and even of local rules, between one nation and another; nations may even disagree over the conundrums posed by gender. Lord Killanin in his own contribution shows that the definition of amateurism is a tricky business, and no answer that satisfies everyone is likely to be found. Take the case of association football. At one time the Olympic competition was a kind of amateur equivalent to the World Cup; now it has been wholly spoiled, because Communist doublethink counts as amateurs *all* the footballers of certain East European countries, whose notion of amateurism is by no means the same as ours.

Besides internationalism, Coubertin strongly believed in fair play. Although the Greek athletes were by his standards brutal and unchivalrous, they agreed about and kept the rules. Men with whips stood by the competitors, ready to punish an infringement with instant violence; the modern Olympic authorities, not to mention those at Wembley, Wimbledon and now even Lord's, may well wish they could imitate this practice.

The unpleasantness that so often spoils the enjoyment of modern sport does not arise only from the differences of outlook between nations, or even from exploitation by commercial interests. It is often due to the notion, encouraged by journalists in search of a 'sensation', that sportsmanship and fair play are sentimental nonsense cultivated by an élite of gentlemen in the past, and that true 'professionalism' has no use for such anachronisms. This is as unintelligent as it is ungenerous; for the moment such an attitude becomes widespread, the pleasure of both participants and spectators in any sport is ruined.

21

Food in Antiquity

The great cook Alexis Soyer[1] came to London from his native France after the fall of Charles X, when he was twenty-one years of age. After being employed in various aristocratic houses he became chef to the Reform Club, and in that capacity prepared many famous banquets, including a breakfast for two thousand people on the morning of Queen Victoria's coronation and a grand dinner for Ibrahim Pasha in 1846; an appendix to the book now reviewed, *The Pantropheon*, gives full details of some of these repasts. During the Irish potato famine he did much to alleviate distress by preparing numerous meals in Dublin at half the normal cost. He invented a 'magic stove', which could be placed upon a table to be used; its working was explained in his book *Soyer's Charitable Cooker, or The Poor Man's Regenerator*. After leaving the Reform Club he opened a restaurant in Lady Blessington's former home, Gore House, Kensington, hoping that the Great Exhibition, then about to open in the neighbourhood, would bring him patronage; it did, but he lost £7,000. During the Crimean War he volunteered to go out to the front; with Florence Nightingale he reorganised the victualling of our military hospitals, besides taking charge of the feeding of a whole division of the army.

Soyer is said to have been the original of Alcide Mirobolant, the French cook in *Pendennis*, who arrives at his employer's house in the wake of his library, pictures and grand piano and takes a stroll in the village, wearing 'his light green frock or paletot, his crimson velvet waistcoat, with blue glass buttons, his *pantalon écossais* of a very large and decided check, his orange satin neckcloth and his jean-boots, with tips of shining leather', together with a gold embroidered cap and richly gilt cane. His wife was the delightful and accomplished Emma Jones, stepdaughter of the painter Simoneau, who herself won great

* A review of *The Pantropheon* by Alexis Soyer in *The Times Literary Supplement*, 13 May 1977.

[1] There is an excellent life of Soyer, *Portrait of a Chef* by Helen Morris (1938, reprinted 1980).

success with pictures like 'The Blind Boy', 'The Young Savoyards Resting', 'Taglioni and the English Ceres'. Sadly, she died, at twenty-nine, after prematurely giving birth owing to the shock of a terrible thunderstorm. Soyer himself died in 1858, when not yet fifty years of age.

He found time to write many books, and this photographic reprint of the most famous of them deserves and will receive a most warm welcome. Since its appearance in 1853 our knowledge of most of the topics treated in it has of course advanced. We have an excellent general treatment of the subject in *Food in Antiquity*, by Don and Patricia Brothwell (1969), one a dietician and the other qualified in biology as well as archaeology and anthropology. We have exhaustive treatments of cultivated plants and domestic animals in antiquity by Victor Hehn, of animals in general by Otto Keller and J.M.C. Toynbee, of Greek birds and fishes by Sir D'Arcy Thompson, an eminent biologist as well as an admirable classical scholar; we have the work of K.D. White on Roman farming and its implements, of L.A. Moritz on mills and grain, of Brian Sparkes on Greek kitchen utensils; we have an annotated translation of the Roman cookery book ascribed to Apicius by Barbara Flower and Elisabeth Rosenbaum.

But what Soyer offers is something different, a general account of ancient foodstuffs and everything connected with their preparation. There are odd references to Assyrians, Egyptians and Jews, but naturally, in view of the extent of the material, the Greco-Roman world is given first place. Soyer was not primarily a classical scholar, and the expert will find certain errors. Some readers may be irritated to find a few places called by their French names, so that Brindisi appears as Brindes and Brittany as Bretagne. But the book contains a vast mass of information, supported by many learned references; the writer is specially familiar with his 'beloved masters' Pliny, Apicius, Petronius and Athenaeus. The work is composed in an engaging and highly individual style; and the author's experience enables him to comment upon the matter, from his particular standpoint, with unique authority. It makes delightful reading.

Homer depicts his heroes as feasting upon the flesh of the oxen they looted from their enemies; though Troy is near the best fishing waters of the Mediterranean, fish is never mentioned as part of their diet. But the Greeks of historical times ate abstemiously, as their poverty required; they ate meat only rarely, when some festive occasion had demanded a sacrifice. The Hellenistic age, with its rich kings and mercenaries, produced some notable gourmets. That age is more remarkable for delicacy of taste than for profusion. The didactic epic of Archestratus of Gela, whose opening amusingly parodies the preludes of more pretentious works, is concerned chiefly with the varieties of fish; the most delicious bread, he says, is baked at Eresos in Lesbos, and when Hermes goes shopping for the gods, he calls there with his little basket.

But the Romans, once they had acquired luxurious tastes from the Ptolemies and the Seleucids, went far beyond them both in greed and ostentation. Even Julius Caesar indulged in the disgusting practice of tickling his throat with a feather so as to vomit up what he had eaten and find room for more; a century later, Vitellius would account for a hundred birds at one sitting by this method. Soyer has two brief appendices, in a style recalling Lemprière's, on Nero and Heliogabalus. In a longer appendix he describes some of the great banquets of his own time, usually as an eyewitness; he rightly points out that they were like those of the Romans.

Soyer had far too good taste to sympathise with the worst excesses of the great banqueters. He points out that the giving of such feasts is due not only to greed, but to the love of display, and seeks to excuse the members of his own profession for their part in 'those follies, which cooks were forced to obey'. He does not conceal his own opinions. He has little sympathy with the Roman eaters of fox, ass or asafoetida, or with the Roman parvenus who threw live slaves to conger eels or red mullets to improve their flavour. He rebukes Solon for interfering with other people's pleasure by his sumptuary laws, and counters Seneca's condemnation of cookery with an effective accusation of pedantry and hypocrisy against 'the atrabilious preceptor of Nero'.

The book contains innumerable fascinating facts; a brief selection must suffice. The Pythagoreans like some faddists nowadays, would not eat eggs; Egyptian shepherds, however, boiled these by rapid friction by whirling them in a sling. The French word 'noisette' is derived from the town of Praeneste, near Rome, where hazel-nuts were grown. The practice of hatching chickens in ovens began in ancient Egypt. The earliest writer to mention sugar, during the fourth century BC, calls it a kind of honey. A king of Bithynia was seized in the middle of the night with a strange longing for loaches, and ordered his cook to produce some or perish instantly; the cook, being unable to procure them, served his master with a dish of radishes carefully seasoned, which the king pronounced to be the best loaches he had ever tasted. At one time Mark Antony became so fond of fishing that Cleopatra felt neglected. She sent a diver to hook on to his line a salted sardine, and while he was still unhooking it, exclaimed, 'Leave to Egyptians the task of fishing; Romans should take only kings, cities and emperors'.

22

Aristotle and Greek Tragedy

Housman's low estimate of his classical colleagues as literary critics is strongly borne out by the character of some of the most fashionable handbooks upon Greek tragedy, which still approach the subject from a point of view very like that represented in Shakespearian criticism by Andrew Bradley. A sharp corrective is administered by this remarkable book, whose author taught law before he began teaching English, but has never been a professional classical scholar. The work is imagined by the author as being 'the first part of a trilogy dealing with the presentation of the self in western literature'. It is by no means easy reading, for its style and vocabulary are harsh, technical, and unappealing; and though in many places this style helps the author to express concisely complicated thoughts, there are others where its artificiality introduces unnecessary difficulties. The author's ruthless and lawyer-like demonstration of his thesis seems to me a little over-rigid, as I shall try to show. But he has produced by far the most important critical study of the subject to appear for many years, and any reader with a serious interest in Greek tragedy as literature has no choice but to make the effort which the reading of his book demands. Most of my space must be used to show where I differ from Jones; but the differences between us are far less numerous than the agreements.

The opening section starts by correcting two misapprehensions of the *Poetics* that have led to grave misunderstanding of Aristotle's whole approach to tragedy. Max Kommerell had already shown that the belief that Aristotle thought that every tragedy must have a hero rests on a mistranslation in the thirteenth chapter of the *Poetics* of which even Bywater was guilty.[1] Jones shows how this error has been used to obscure the implications of the statements in the seventh chapter that 'tragedy is an imitation not of human beings but of action and life' and that 'the stage-figures do not act in order to represent

---

* A review of *On Aristotle and Greek Tragedy* by John Jones in *Review of English Studies* n.S. xv, May 1964.

[1] *Lessing und Aristoteles* (1940), p. 160; cf. pp. 189, 228, 293.

their characters; they include their characters for the sake of their actions.' In defiance of these doctrines, the imported concept of the hero has been used to interpret tragedy in terms of an interest in individual character that is altogether modern. Having done much to elucidate Aristotle's theory, Jones goes on to examine the extant plays in the light of his results.

At the start he is encouraged by the observation that the lack of individuation in the characters of the *Suppliant Women* of Aeschylus helped to maintain the belief in its early date, almost universal from the beginning of this century until the publication of new evidence in 1952 showed that it was almost certainly written after the *Persians* and the *Seven Against Thebes*. Aeschylus' art was thought to have developed from naïve beginnings represented by the *Suppliant Women* to the comparatively advanced characterisation which the *Oresteia*, performed two years before his death, was supposed to show. This view of the *Oresteia* is strongly disputed by Jones, who believes it to be concerned hardly at all with the individual members of the House of Atreus, almost entirely with the House itself and the reestablishment of its normal existence which has been disturbed by the usurpation of Agamemnon's murderers. Jones allows even the characters of the *Oresteia* the smallest possible degree of individuality; he shows convincingly how modern critics' interest in individuals has blinded them to much of the effect of the play as a whole, and he justly complains that both those who make out Agamemnon as a hybristic tyrant and those who regard him as a perfect gentleman 'operate at the same level of individualistic humanism'.

Jones finds fault with those who have applied the word 'primitive' to Aeschylus' thought; but he himself has been carried too far by his anthropological approach to Aeschylus' characters, a few of whom do reveal the beginnings of individual portrayal. The basic principle of *ethos*, the word which in ancient literary criticism roughly corresponds to our word 'character', is that the persons in a story should have the qualities which their actions presuppose. A few of Aeschylus' characters act in a way that seems to presuppose both good and bad qualities; and this mixed nature is clearly indicated in their presentation. Two such characters are Agamemnon in the *Oresteia* and Eteocles in the *Seven Against Thebes*. Agamemnon is both the brave king and warrior and the accursed son of Oedipus. Both have to be made comparatively sympathetic; and the disastrous errors of judgment which they make are explained in Homeric terms by saying that in virtue of the curse they have inherited Zeus has sent Ate, the spirit of destruction, to take away their wits. Agamemnon is neither wholly good nor wholly bad, but has elements of both, as he has in Homer, of whose all-pervasive influence on early tragedy Jones seems not sufficiently aware. In exalting the importance of the House of Atreus, he underrates that of the individual heroes who are its members, which is as real for Aeschylus as it was for Homer. The double character of these two kings seems to me to have obliged the poet to give them a more distinct individuality than his other characters.[2] Clytemnestra, says Jones, 'stands outside the norm'; her abnormal qualities have been given her not for their own sake, but because her actions require that she possess them. This is both true and important and it is true of other characters beside Clytemnestra; but because Clytemnestra's striking characteristics are not there for their own sake, but for the sake of the action, it does not follow that the poet is not free to exploit them to secure subsidiary effects; and when in Jones's words 'a modern sensibility snatches hungrily at the touches of reckless moral autonomy ... which Aeschylus bestows on her', it has rather more justification in doing so than Jones allows.

'Sophocles' achievement,' says Jones, speaking of his treatment of individual character, 'was to realise privacy'; 'in the place of family solidarity,' he writes, 'we have individuation and (in a vague provisional sense) personalising of consciousness.' Sophocles's work certainly shows a development in this direction, but a rather less abrupt development than Jones allows; for example, his comparison of Sophocles' treatment of the revenge of Orestes in his *Electra* with Aeschylus' handling of the same story in *The Libation-Bearers* sometimes lays a wrong emphasis on the differences between them. Aeschylus' play is part of a trilogy, but Sophocles' an independent drama in which he chose to concentrate attention on the figure of Electra, whose heroic nature is revealed in her clashes with her sister and her mother. Like those of Aeschylus, the characters of Sophocles reveal no idiosyncrasy, but the more important ones are given a distinct individuality, always in a manner suitable to the requirements of the action. It is indeed wrong to say (or to think that Aristotle said) that every play must have a hero in the sense of a central figure around whom everything revolves. But every complete play of Sophocles does contain a figure of heroic stature, whose character is deliberately contrasted with those of ordinary mortals. Sometimes the hero stands out in contrast with his enemies, like Ajax, Philoctetes, or Electra in relation to Clytemnestra; sometimes an obvious foil for him is created, as Ismene for Antigone, Chrysothemis for Electra; Creon's relation to Oedipus in the *Oedipus Tyrannus* has something in common with both

---

[2] For Agamemnon, see *CQ*, n.s. xii (1962), 187 and for Eteocles, *Gnomon* xxxiv (1962), 740.

these types. Yet always character is subordinate to plot and action, and this important fact Jones admirably demonstrates. His section about Sophocles is full of acute observations and profound insights. Here, in particular, one regrets the brevity of the book, for with more space available it could have contained more of the analysis of particular sections of the texts that is best exemplified by his excellent treatment of an episode in the *Philoctetes* (pp. 162f.); best of all is the chapter called 'Men and Mutability'. I believe that he underrates the *Ajax* through a failure to understand it; that he mistakenly neglects the important part played in the second Oedipus play by what is going on at Thebes; and that he mistakes the nature of Antigone, to which the family curse (see 582f., and cf. *Electra*, 515f.) is relevant in a way recalling Agamemnon and Eteocles in Aeschylus.

The section about Euripides is on a smaller scale than the rest, and is less satisfying. If Sophocles attained privacy, Euripides according to Jones attained inwardness; he instances some of the many passages in which a character is shown debating with himself about the merits of a proposed course of action and inclining now one way and now the other. His favourite example is the perplexity of Agamemnon at the opening of the *Iphigenia in Aulis* as he debates whether or not he shall entice his daughter to Aulis by a trick so that she may be sacrificed. Euripides, like Aeschylus, liked to exploit dilemmas such as that of Agamemnon at Aulis or that of Orestes when he had to decide whether or not to kill his mother. Aeschylus, as was natural for a writer of his date, gave a theological explanation for the decisions of his characters; he could say that Zeus sent Ate to take away Agamemnon's wits so that he sacrificed his daughter, or that Apollo told Orestes that he must kill his mother. Euripides was not concerned to deny the existence of the gods (a fact clearly realised by Jones, who has no sympathy with the popular notion of this poet as a propagandist); but he preferred to get his effects by showing different passions at work within the human mind and struggling with each other to influence its decision. Whether these passions are or are not implanted by the gods is of no special consequence, though it is worth observing that in some plays, in the *Hippolytus* for instance, the poet tells us that they are. Euripides certainly shows an access of interest in the human passions, and not only in their effects, but in their detailed workings. But this does not justify the somewhat vague statement that he shows an access of interest in human beings, or in human consciousness. When he presents the consciousness at work, it is always either registering impressions that conform to certain standard types (even in Alcestis' death scene, which is here misrepresented through failure to recognise the convention) or debating a course of action by presenting arguments on both sides. Nowhere does the poet show the slightest interest in human idiosyncrasy; certainly not in connection with the farmer to whom Aegisthus marries Electra in the *Electra*. Characters of humble status but of heroic virtue were familiar to the fifth-century audience, which knew well the part played in the *Odyssey* by Eumaeus and Philoetius; although poor, the farmer is of good birth; and as the trial scene in the *Orestes* indicates, Euripides had good reasons for showing his partiality for honest farmers. The debates of Euripidean characters with themselves, like their innumerable debates with one another, are never far removed from rhetoric. Does their author show more interest in human beings than Sophocles, whose characters, for all their lack of idiosyncrasy, are more vivid and better able to arouse our sympathies? Sophocles' form is perfectly adapted to his matter, so that his characters seem to speak with the straightforward utterance of passion.

The main thesis of this book, that Greek tragedy must be understood not in terms of character but in terms of plot and action, seems to me to have been demonstrated with triumphant success; a major factor in that success is the author's understanding of the religious outlook of early Greece and his freedom from the usual tendency to interpolate modern religious notions. Most modern presentations of the subject err in exaggerating the accessibility of Greek tragedy to our understanding. Jones supplies a valuable corrective, but has gone a little too far in the opposite direction. 'It turns out to be our bad luck,' he writes on the last page but one, 'that Greek tragedy is superficially intelligible in a modern way.' That sentence might almost imply that the fifth-century Greeks inhabited a world of thought mysteriously different from our own, like that of primitive savages whose cast of mind is strangely remote from that of normal civilised beings. If instead of crudely assimilating the early Greek world outlook to one or other of those familiar to ourselves we are willing to start again from scratch and make a careful and dispassionate investigation of the data bearing on it that we possess, there is no reason why we should approach with undue despondency the effort needed to enter in imagination into the state of mind necessary in order to understand Greek tragedy. Jones's book has done a good deal to increase our prospect of success.

23

Kott's Greek Tragedy

The notion that the world of the Greek tragedians is as strange and alien to modern men as that of the most remote and savage tribes has done harm in recent years. But there is no excuse for the reaction against it that assures us that Greek tragedy is somehow the same as almost everything else – Christianity, Marxism, Existentialism, Structuralism – and can be merged with all these into some tasteless mixture like *The Eating of the Gods*. Having persuaded many readers, including several actors and producers, who respect his authority as he does theirs, that Shakespeare is our contemporary, Jan Kott has now set out to do the same for Aeschylus, Sophocles and Euripides.

The book's content is not easy to describe; Professor Kott's excited, breathless manner does not make for clarity, and his eagerness to compare or equate as many different civilisations, literatures and religions as he can keeps causing one thing to get in the way of another. But a few main points come across. The *Prometheus* is ambiguous because in it two different kinds of time coexist; Prometheus both wins and loses. Until Professor Kott, everyone has thought the second half of Sophocles' *Ajax* to be a bore, but he has shown that it presents the end of the Heroic Age. The Alcestis who returns from the grave is and is not Alcestis; when Admetus takes the Stranger by the hand, 'her hand is icy'. A long chapter about various tragic presentations of Heracles brings out the points he had in common with Christ; Heracles might say, like Frank Harris: 'He may have gone deeper, but I have touched life at more points.' In the chapter on the *Bacchae* which gives the book its name, the comparison with a medieval miracle-play once more looms large, and the defunct theory, massacred by Pickard-Cambridge in 1927 (we should read the real *Dithyramb, Tragedy and Comedy* of 1927, not the travesty presented as a 'second edition' in 1962) lives again. So does Gilbert Murray's unfortunate theory that Orestes and Hamlet are somehow the same,

* A review of *The Eating of the Gods* by Jan Kott in *The Times Literary Supplement,* 29 November 1974.

though it must be said in fairness that Professor Kott does not add that it is because both stand for the Corn Spirit.

Readers need not be afraid of finding Professor Kott excessively encumbered with Greek learning, but they will be comforted by much dropping of fashionable names; most pages contain a sentence like 'Martin Heidegger was the first to analyse this anxiety of human existence in the Chorus of *Antigone* as being part of man's condition' or ' "There is significance in rebelling," Mao writes in his Red Book'. But such ideas as the book contains are as novel as the dodo, and about as much alive; defunct speculations of Victorian anthropology are given a surface gloss.

When Professor Kott saw Hamlet performed at Elsinore, 'during the first soliloquy some gulls flew just above Hamlet's head, and a couple of them suddenly squatted at his feet'. This is only one of many equally trivial observations that seem important to the author of this tiresome, silly and pretentious book, my copy of which any gull is welcome to use for any purpose.

24

A Failure to Face up to Tragedy

Greek poetry is a force in the modern world, not simply on account of pious antiquarianism. Like all the greatest artists, the early Greek poets were concerned not with problems that were important only for their own time, but with problems that are permanent, because they result from the basic situation of human beings, limited by mortality and human weakness, but able to imagine and aspire to noble ideals. Their religion makes only modest claims for men. Men were created only by a minor god, Prometheus, and have no special claim upon divine favour; the gods rule in their own interest, as men would if they were the rulers, and allow men only a modest share of happiness. Zeus does men a kindness by seeing to it that in the end their crimes against each other will be punished, even if the punishment falls not on the criminal himself, but on his descendants. But the chains of guilt and punishment may be too complicated for men to recognize the workings of divine justice; the mind of Zeus is inscrutable to men. The noblest among men try, in the face of the limitations imposed upon them by their human status, to live by standards of honour not unlike those of the gods. For a mortal to do this means running great risks; but what matters most to such a man is honour, and he is content if he can vindicate his claim to it, even if he can do so only in the moment of annihilation.

Since the decline of belief in Christianity this outlook has seemed, at least to people who can understand it, peculiarly relevant to the human situation; it is significant that the first person to point out its relevance has had vast influence on modern thought. That person is Nietzsche, whose work has affected indirectly even people who have never read him and imagine him to have been a proto-Nazi; his full importance is now beginning to be realized, even in this country. It is by no means only writers who have had classical education who illustrate this interest in Greek religion; the two best examples that occur to me are those of Conrad and of Lawrence, whose general view of life has much in common with the attitude that has been described.

Some writers have shown their awareness of the special relevance of the Greek outlook to the modern predicament by making use of Greek myths; these have furnished the subject-matter of a number of successful modern dramas. But in this country, at least, modern productions of Greek plays have usually been disappointing. Between about 1910 and 1930 Gilbert Murray's translations of Greek plays, into sub-Swinburnian romantic verse had great success. Apart from what now seems the grotesque inappropriateness of the medium, these works rested on a view of early Greek thinking untouched by the considerations just outlined. Murray identified the attitude of the Greek poets, particularly his favourite Euripides, with his own liberalism; Euripides' depiction of the horrors of the Trojan War seemed to him to be a protest against militarism and imperialism. But Euripides cannot have doubted that the Trojans, if they had won, would have acted just as the Greeks acted; he was concerned not with the belief in human perfectibility but with permanent features of human behaviour, not likely to change while human nature remained the same.

Since Murray's versions went out of favour, the decline of rhyme and the popularity of blank verse have made things easier for translators of Greek poetry. There are some good modern translations of Greek plays; most of these come from America, but perhaps the best of all is Louis MacNeice's rendering of Aeschylus' *Agamemnon*. Also the vast difference between Greek and modern theatrical conventions has come to seem less of an impediment to understanding than it did when it was generally assumed that dramatic productions should always aim at naturalism; in the age of Brecht and Beckett, an age, too, in which radio and television have familiarized audiences with the idea that different kinds of drama may have different conventions, the peculiar nature of Greek stage conventions has a better chance of being understood. All the same, most modern productions of Greek plays have been disappointing.

One reason is that a Greek play is written to be acted in a Greek theatre. Apart from the actors, it has a chorus, which separates off the acts with lyric utterances. In a Greek theatre the actors are on a raised stage, the chorus in a wide space in front of the stage called the orchestra; there is interaction between the actors and the chorus but the two areas must be distinct. The country where the best productions of ancient Greek plays are to be seen is Greece itself. This is partly because they take place in actual ancient theatres of the kind for which the plays were written, though it is also because Greek actors are far better than English ones at expressing strong emotions.

One way of dealing with this difficulty is to adapt Greek plays to the requirements of the modern theatre. John Barton achieved great success with a series of Shakespeare's history plays, modified and in places even amplified to suit his requirements, and he has now fitted together adaptations of nine plays and certain parts of the *Iliad* to give a more or less continuous narrative of events from the sacrifice of Iphigeneia at Aulis, just before the Trojan War, to her rescue by her brother from the Crimea some seven years after it. Apart from the great distinction of his work in the theatre, Mr Barton is a highly cultivated man who was once a don at Cambridge, and could have become a distinguished scholar, as well as the husband of one. Unfortunately he does not know Greek; but he has had the assistance of Mr Kenneth Cavander, who won high academic honours in classics at Oxford before entering the theatrical and literary world. Both men's qualifications demand that their work should receive critical attention, the more so since it has been performed by a company of great professional skill.

No sensible person would require that the plays should be treated reverentially, as they too often have been in the past. Great harm has been done in the past by the cliché, reiterated in the United States in its most tiresome form by Francis Fergusson, that the plays were part of a religious ritual. In a sense the thing is true, but it was a ritual of a religion not at all like Christianity, though less unlike the Catholicism of Southern Europe or the Orthodox religion of the Greeks than it is unlike the Protestantism of Northern Europe. The religious element did not mean that the element of enjoyment was not important; the atmosphere of a village *festa* in southern Italy or a village *paneyiri* in Greece, though very different, gives a better notion of what it must have been like than an English service or oratorio. It is greatly to the credit of the adapters that they have kept clear of this mistake.

It is even more to their credit that they never try to assimilate Greek religion to Christianity. They know that the early Greeks thought of the world as a hard world, in which men could expect only occasional favours from the gods; at the same time they know that, though remote and awful, the gods are not unjust. This is so important, and it is still so rare to find it properly understood, that they deserve very great credit for being so well aware of it.

Still, the gods are not awe-inspiring enough and the heroes are not sufficiently heroic. Since Rousseau's time modern man has tried more and more to abolish the notion of being responsible for his actions; he is caught up in a chain of circumstances for which society is to blame and he can get through life only by behaving as a member of a group and so saving himself the burden of decision. The early Greeks felt that even if human beings were not wholly responsible for their actions, at least they ought to behave as if they were. That attitude has greatly affected the interpretation of Greek tragedy, especially that of Euripides; and some of it can be seen here.

The obvious difficulty in the way of such an enterprise is that it involves fitting together into a continuous whole works of very different mood, temper and artistic purpose. It is true that seven of the ten works which have served as primary models are by one author, Euripides. But Euripides by no means always wrote in the same key. The *Hecuba* and *Trojan Women* are grim depictions of human suffering at its most intense; the *Helen* and the *Iphigeneia in Tauris* are lyrical dramas describing the escape of heroines from captivity in distant lands; the *Iphigeneia in Aulis, Orestes* and *Andromache* are exciting plays with much action and frequent change, having elements of sadness but issuing in endings which in general may be called happy. With these Mr Barton has combined three works by poets even greater than Euripides, all invested with the high seriousness of true tragedy. In these varied works, it often happens that the same character is treated very differently, and that the same action is viewed under different aspects. The adapters have tried to deal with this difficulty partly by excisions and additions, and partly by confining themselves to two ways of treating a play; some plays and some characters are treated seriously, while others are burlesqued, not always with fortunate results.

One factor tending to mold the diverse material together is the adapters' language. The language of Greek tragedy, particularly of its extensive lyric elements, is uncommonly rich and varied, hardly less than that of Shakespeare. As Mr Barton argues in his programme note, some of the language of tragedy is taut and spare, and this element has received less than its due from some translators. But much of the language is splendid and ornate; and of that the hearer of this production will get no idea. The language of Mr Barton and Mr Cavander is flat, colloquial, matter-of-fact, even in those places where the text is based on lyric verse in the originals. It does not often descend to the vulgar bathos of Agamemnon's 'My mind is full of pressures' or Hermione's 'Because I'm not pregnant, they say I'm no good in bed', but it has few positive qualities, and one might sit through a performance without suspecting that the original was written in great poetry. Occasionally, when the adapters are content to translate the original literally, poetry does come through, notably the poetry of Homer and Aeschylus.

To be squeezed into the continuous narrative, all the works used have had to be cut considerably, and they have lost much of their individuality in the process. The operation has been performed with great dexterity; but the hearer familiar with the originals will miss much, he will note some very undistinguished additions, and he will be angered by frequent failures of taste.

It would not be proper, even if it were practicable, to restrict the right of writers and producers to adapt the work of predecessors to their own requirements. But when one sets out to adapt great works of art, certain risks are unavoidable; some people may feel that the new product fails to justify the liberties taken with the old. The main defect of this adaptation lies in a very English unwillingness to face up to tragedy without varying it with light entertainment suitable to the English sense of humour, without playing up to the English distrust of strong emotion by 'sending up' the serious poetry with interludes of burlesque. The Aldwych audience is clearly delighted with the production, and especially with the burlesque elements; and if the satisfaction of the public is the touchstone of excellence, then it is a great success. But I must regretfully say that I found the burlesque silly, vulgar and in execrable taste, and that most people who know the originals will share this feeling.

First comes the 'trilogy' called *The War* (two and a half hours); this uses Euripides' *Iphigeneia in Aulis*, episodes from Homer's *Iliad*, and Euripides' *Trojan Women*. The chorus, which the adapters have reduced to the level of mere commentators on the action, poses them a grave problem. What in the original are continuous lyric utterances of great beauty and profundity have been split up between various speakers; presented in this way, much of their content sounds banal and unnecessary.

The chorus gives the show a bad start with a rambling and jocose account of the beginning of things, delivered with much simpering and giggling. But the heroic sacrifice of Iphigeneia comes over well, despite the unheroic Achilles of Mike Gwilym, the shrewish Clytemnestra of Janet Suzman, and an Agamemnon played throughout by John Shrapnel as though he were the bumbling paterfamilias of a soap opera about businessmen. The scenes based on the *Iliad* have one or two distressing features. Before the quarrel with Achilles, Chryseis goes through the tired ritual of erotic massage upon the bourgeois Agamemnon rather as Miss Rita Chevrolet might be imagined to do for Lord Gnome; Thetis is depicted as a jazzy blonde, whose looks are well calculated to embarrass her son in the way the hero of Iolanthe is embarrassed by his fairy mother's. (This is surely the producer's fault; the reviewer cannot say anything disrespectful about Miss Annie Lambert, whose stunning performance on the box as Zelda enchanted even old and desiccated philologists.) But the scenes based on Homer are surprisingly successful. Mr Barton in the programme note says that the tragedians avoided these episodes as subject matter out of respect for Homer. He is wrong; they supplied material for one of Aeschylus' most famous trilogies, from which a marvellous speech by Achilles has been discovered on a papyrus. Homer was the chief inspiration of the tragedians, and the presentation of these episodes brings out his strong dramatic quality. Least successful though, is Priam's visit to Achilles's tent to recover his son's body; Priam is insufficiently infirm and Achilles insufficiently ferocious.

The *Trojan Women* episode too goes well; Eliza Ward is a good, though a too youthful, Hecuba, and that superb actress Billie Whitelaw is well cast as Andromache. But one great scene miscarries, that in which Hecuba denounces Helen before Menelaus. This scene is truly tragic, for though Hecuba's claim that Helen has caused the disaster by yielding to her passion commands sympathy, Helen's plea that she was overborne by the power of Aphrodite must be taken seriously. This effect is lost because Janet Suzman plays Helen as a frivolous and hard-hearted siren, which is not what Euripides intended. But in this production Helen and Menelaus are marked out for comic treatment, so that any tragic scenes involving them can hardly be successful.

Part Two is called *The Murders* (two and a half hours); its first episode is based on Euripides' *Hecuba*, its second on Aeschylus' *Agamemnon*, and its third on Sophocles' *Electra*, with some matter from Euripides' *Electra*. The first starts badly with a pert and mincing Polyxena, instead of the great opening with the ghost of Polydorus; but the Polymestor episode does not fail of its effect. The *Agamemnon* is miserably truncated, and in the case of this masterpiece, an infinitely greater work than anything by Euripides, the usual errors of taste jar more than ever. Agamemnon enters on a chariot drawn by Trojan female prisoners: one expects him to begin. 'Holla, ye pampered jades of Asia!'

Clytemnestra is played by Miss Suzman as a hollow and brittle good-time cutie; during a scene in which she persuades Agamemnon to make a triumphant entry over the tapestries, she sits perched on the yoke of the chariot instead of standing in the doorway to confront him. When Clytemnestra in the bitterest of all her speeches says that Iphigeneia will meet her father by the river of Acheron and will throw her arm round him and kiss him, the adapters find it necessary to add the words 'if she can'. But in spite of all this, something of the greatness of the *Agamemnon* comes through.

In the *Electra* episode the combination of materials from as many as four different works does not make for unity. Since Lynn Dearth, in spite of having to act with Miss Suzman, who when she wants to seem passionate only seems bad-tempered, plays Electra with real passion, an unnecessary touch of vulgarity can be forgiven her; Mike Gwilym makes up for his unheroic Achilles by his fine Orestes. The moment of the recognition of Orestes by his sister, acted by these two performers, is perhaps the finest of the whole production. So on the whole the Electra episode succeeds, though here too lapses of taste occur. In the original, after the fictitious death of Orestes has been described, Clytemnestra's first reaction is one of sorrow. The messenger expresses disappointment that the news he brings has not, after all, proved welcome; but Clytemnestra quickly reassures him. The incident has tragic quality, provided one recognizes that Clytemnestra's first reaction is not to be written off as insincere; but Miss Suzman plays the scene in a way that shows that she is unaware of this.

Part Three is called *The Gods* (three hours); it is made up out of four plays of Euripides, the *Helen*, the *Orestes*, the *Andromache* and the *Iphigeneia in Tauris*. In the first of these, disaster strikes; the spirit of Offenbach's *La Belle Hélène* has vanquished the spirit of Euripides' play and driven it from the field. Helen is presented as a Noel Coward heroine, brittle, jolly, scatter-brained, a bit of a vamp but essentially nice, saving the pathetically comic Menelaus from the lustful Turk Theoclymenus with his Arab costume and ferocious whiskers. Of course Miss Suzman is just right for this. The real *Helen* is a lyrical drama of haunting beauty; it inspired Goethe in the Helen episode of the second part of Faust, as the Tauric *Iphigeneia* inspired him in the *Iphigenie*.

Miss Suzman's Noel Coward-type Helen carries over into the *Orestes*, and since in that play Helen is less sympathetically portrayed, she is wholly out of key. But the *Orestes* on the whole goes well, though disappointingly the most baroque passage in all Euripides, the lyric monody describing the attempted kidnapping of Helen, is taken from the Phrygian eunuch and given to a female; it says much for the respectability of the Royal Shakespeare Company that evidently no male actor could be found who was suitable to play the eunuch's role. At the end, Orestes and Electra suddenly turn into Andreas Baader and Ulrike Meinhof, and start shooting off guns in all directions, till they are calmed down by a bearded, middle-aged, greying Apollo. But the real horror comes when the burlesque treatment of the *Helen* spills over into the *Andromache*. The original play begins with Andromache with her young son desperately seeking sanctuary at an altar. The window of Hector has been carried off to Greece as the concubine of Achilles' son Neoptolemus, by whom she has had a son. In her master's absence, she is in mortal danger from the bitter jealousy of his childless legitimate wife Hermione and her father Menelaus; in the end she is rescued by her master's aged grandfather, Peleus. This deeply moving episode is here turned into farce; Hermione appears in the impossibly tight dress of a cocotte of the Second Empire, does a strip-tease, and has her bottom smacked; the golden-hearted gruffness of Peleus is unbearable; Thetis reappears, with saccharine effect. In spite of these vulgarities, Miss Whitelaw contrives to give a real notion of the pathos of the genuine Andromache; only an actress of very high quality could have done this.

Then, when all seems lost, honour is retrieved by the *Iphigeneia in Tauris* episode, which is beautiful and moving. Iphigeneia and the chorus look splendid in Russian costume, reminding one of Garbo in *Ninotchka*; the great scene of the recognition of Orestes by his sister comes over well; and in spite of being costumed like an abbess, without helm or aegis, Miss Whitelaw provides a wonderful finale, bringing solace in noble words from the *Eumenides* of Aeschylus. Not that Aeschylus ever said that hate and love were the same thing, or anything so silly.

For people who do not know the originals, this entertainment offers a means of getting a very rough idea of the character of Greek tragedy which is better than any they have been offered for some time; when one remembers the travesty of the *Oresteia* recently inflicted from the goggle-box, one is thankful for the new work. But people who know Greek would be wise to stay away.

25

Steiner's 'Babel'

George Steiner seems almost too eloquent and well-informed to be real, a sort of literary equivalent of Baron Arnheim in Robert Musil's *Der Mann ohne Eigenschaften*. Brought up in Paris and New York by German-speaking parents and speaking from the start French, English and German, but with Czech and Hebrew present in the background, he is a truly international man of letters. He is at home with the literatures of his three main languages; he is familiar with modern philosophy and linguistics, both the Continental and the Anglo-American sort; and he has the power to assimilate and communicate the data of sciences seldom accessible to literary men. His English is not that of an Englishman, nor yet that of an American. I find in it little French but much German influence; yet it is not the ordinary Germanic English of the transatlantic *Gelehrter*. He belongs to what he has called 'the German tradition of philosophic amplitude'; the reader must understand the dialectical movement of his thought, in which thesis is followed by antithesis and antithesis by synthesis. His utterance is voluble, polysyllabic, full of quotations from and allusions to a wide range of authors.

Confronted with so much erudition and so much ebullience, the English reader's first reaction is often one of alarm. He complains of name-dropping; he points to sentences that seem to him pretentious. He shrinks back before such stern determination to classify all phenomena according to philosophic categories; and he protests in the name of common sense and empirical method against what he finds to be a luxuriant indulgence in metaphysical theorising. Yet if he is an intelligent specimen of his kind and if he persists in reading, he will change his mind. Professor Steiner is not only a widely-read and very clever man, but he has a great quantity of solid common sense; the reader who has grasped the peculiar movement of his thinking must recognise that the judgments he arrives at are for the most part singularly sound. It is sad for him that he did not live in the sixteenth

* A review of *After Babel* by George Steiner in *Encounter*, June 1975.

or seventeenth century. In our time a style such as his way of thinking demands must become discoloured by the technical vocabularies of the various disciplines whose data its owner has assimilated. Three centuries ago it was possible for Robert Burton – of whom Professor Steiner's work has always reminded me – exhaustively to anatomise an interesting mental condition in a poetic prose of high quality. In our time this is much harder; but despite certain infelicities Professor Steiner has an individual and distinguished style, and this contributes to the pleasure of reading him.

After Babel is not an account of the Russian short story since the First World War, but is nothing less than an anatomy of translation. Its structure is not easily grasped (a table of contents like that given by Burton would have helped the reader greatly). Professor Steiner's dialectical approach obliges him to start by placing the problem of translation in the setting afforded by the general problem of language; almost half the book is devoted to this task.

Language itself poses varied and complex problems. It is dependent upon human physiology, and its existence is in time; as Logan Pearsall Smith sadly reflected, 'even words must perish'. There are in use some four or five thousand languages, and Professor Steiner gives intriguing details about some of them. My favourite is Kung, a dialect of the Kalahari bushmen that consists largely of clicks and sharp intakes of breath; so far it has resisted phonetic transcription. It is not easy for a person who knows no language that is not Indo-European to understand the enormous difference that can separate one language from another. In studying Japanese one is forced to recognise that what one had lazily assumed to be fundamental categories of human thought are merely local habits. Even inside a language, speech can very immensely according to the sex, age, or status of the speaker. In Japanese there is a word for '*I*' used only in the peculiar language of imperial rescripts, and used there only to denote the Emperor. In that country the language used in letters differs markedly from the language of life, and the language of women from that of men. Japanese has different words for the existential and copulative senses of the verb 'to be'. Having learned some during the war, I set out in an essay for my tutor to refute St Anselm's ontological argument for the existence of God by showing the difficulty of expressing it in that language.

The myth of Babel interestingly attests the belief in an *Ursprache*, a primitive language at the root of all extant languages. Behind much of the history of linguistics one may discern the aspiration to undo the act of God which checked the builders of the tower. That same Leibniz who seems to have been the first to argue that extant

languages actually determine the thinking of their speakers was also
i.e., > the first to project a universal semantic system, which all men would
mathematics understand. Wilhelm von Humboldt saw language as a 'third
universe' midway between empirical reality and the internalised
structures of consciousness. His theory is essentially 'monadist',
holding that different languages generate different pictures of reality.
Yet as Professor Steiner observes he leaves the door open to a
universalising interpretation, which would admit an element common
to the manner in which all languages shape reality.

In our own time Benjamin Lee Whorf, whose volume of essays
Language, Thought and Reality appeared in 1956, argued in detail for the
view that different language systems give rise to different pictures of
the world. Steiner writes with sympathy of this now unfashionable
view, perhaps because of his awareness that bilinguals (or even
people who know a foreign language fairly well) do not translate
literally between languages and do not feel towards the equivalent
words of those languages as though they were precisely equal to each
other. Even between languages of similar structure, one/one
correspondence does not exist.

Few linguists at present sympathise with Whorf; most accept the
universalising theory associated with the generative grammar of
Noam Chomsky. The 'universal deep structures' which generate
language must not be sought, Chomsky explains, at the phonological
or ordinary syntactic level. They are located 'far beyond the level of
C's "project" actual or even potential consciousness'. Progress in locating them has
is now in not so far been impressive; and Steiner after a careful discussion
disrepute; it remarks truly that 'the ancient controversy between relativist and
achieved universalist philosophies of language is not yet over'. Those Marxist
nothing. critics who have complained that Chomsky is simply reviving an
obsolete dogma of 'innate ideas'[1] certainly deserve an answer. Steiner
concludes that general linguistics will not at present help us to attain an
adequate model of translation. A science of language does not yet exist;
and he justly exposes the 'covert distaste for literature' of those modern
critics who search for 'objective' criteria of poetic exegesis and of those
scientific linguists who resent the 'mobile, perhaps anarchic prodigality
of natural forms'.

In his third chapter, which bears the Quinian title of 'Word Against
Object', Steiner considers his subject in terms of four successive
dualities: *one/many; material/immaterial; public/private; true/false.* He
informs us about the physical determinants of speech, about language
in relation to past and future, and about the philosophical problem of

[1] See, for example, S. Timpanaro, *Sul materialismo* (1970).

private language. The difference between the public and private associations of words brings him to the breakdown of ordinary language for literary purposes, which he thinks was foreshadowed by Hölderlin and Gérard de Nerval, came into the open with Rimbaud and Mallarmé, and was made explicit by Hofmannsthal in his *Chandos Letter* of 1902. From the ultra-private new languages which this generated he passes to the search for an ultra-public new universal language that started with the decline of Latin in the seventeenth century. He rightly concludes that neither this nor the logico-analytic notations of modern philosophers has done much to deepen our understanding of natural language or to modify its use. Still more interesting is his survey of language from the aspect of truth in contrast with fiction. After giving an account of the modern discussion of the philosophical problem of truth, Steiner protests against the logicians' and linguists' insistence on viewing falsity only under its negative aspect. Nietzsche, he reminds us, said that we needed lies in order to vanquish the cruel reality of the world; the plurality of language must be vindicated against the restrictive force of unifying systems.

This takes us to a point halfway through the book. The English empiricist will feel that he would have taken for granted the somewhat negative result of the enquiry so far without going over all the ground he has traversed with Steiner. But he must acknowledge that the conclusions reached are very much those which he himself would be willing to accept, and will hope that the argument will convince other readers of different philosophical sympathies.

Now follows a 60-page chapter on 'The Claims of Theory.' Of the various general theories surveyed the most helpful is that of John Dryden, who distinguishes literal translation, free translation and an intermediate kind. Goethe offers a similar tripartite scheme, but relates each of his three types of translation to a different phase in a nation's cultural development. It might be more useful to modify Dryden's scheme not by introducing the notion of chronology, but by using that of purpose. A translation made simply to communicate a factual content will tend to literalism; one made for purely literary purposes will tend to freedom; one made for mixed purposes will tend to belong to the intermediate kind.

Some literary translators interested in content have evolved a systematic method of literal translation, by which words and phrases are constantly rendered in the same way. Steiner curiously fails to mention the first important European translation, the version of the Old Testament known as the Septuagint that was made by Alexandrian Jews during the third century BC, according to tradition on the orders of King Ptolemy Philadelphus. The Aramaic and Greek terminology of translation used by contemporary writers with reference to this work fits with his insistence that translation is itself a kind of interpretation.[2] Yet the translators closely followed the wording of the original. The medieval translators of Aristotle rendered him so closely and so consistently that it has proved possible to restore a lost Greek manuscript from a Latin version with every confidence that the restoration is correct.[3]

Poetry offers difficulty to the translator which prose, unless it is markedly poetical prose, seldom presents. But not all poetical translations are free renderings. Steiner quotes Dante, Rilke, and Nabokov as defenders of a literal method. Hölderlin's translation of Pindar, which was not published in the poet's lifetime, is so literal that it has been debated whether it was really intended as a translation, and not as a kind of crib made for the writer's private use. Steiner rightly regards it as a remarkable translation; but he does not remark what seems to me a fact of great interest, that despite its fidelity to the original it remains, like all its author's work, profoundly German and romantic. The literal method has produced few satisfying renderings of poetry – Browning's *Agamemnon* (which Steiner discusses at some length) and Nabokov's *Eugene Onegin* (the famous attack on it by Edmund Wilson is not mentioned here) are cases in point. On the whole it remains true that a translation of a poem is either a bad poem or an unfaithful rendering. Steiner discusses a translation by Rilke of a poem by the sixteenth-century writer Louise Labé. Rilke's version is, as Steiner says, a 'more important' poem than the original; but the peculiar charm and naivety of the original is not rendered. Rilke's version is his own, and is a thing of beauty. But one cannot help feeling that his action in writing it is in questionable taste. Since antiquity poets have claimed the right to make what they can of other poet's work. But if they make use of it, they run the risk of exciting this kind of feeling.

Steiner's discussion of theories ends with a commendably sceptical conclusion: he thinks the hope expressed by modern theorists of 'a progressive systematisation, of an advance from local inventory and insight to generality and theoretic stability' is a delusion. A careful discussion, with much neuro-physiological detail, of the possibility of a theory of language leads him to conclude that without a theory of

---

[2] See G. Zuntz, *Opuscula Selecta* (1772), 128f.

[3] See R. Kassel, *Der Text der Aristotelischen Rhetorik* (1971), 70, referring to B. Schneider, *Die mittelalterlichen griechisch-lateinischen Übersetzungen der Aristotelischen Rhetorik* (1971).

MRI scans have shown that nouns (& numbers), verbs, & syntax reside in different areas of the frontal lobes.

language there can be no theory of translation.

The practical section of the book begins at p. 296; 118 pages on 'The Hermeneutic Movement' are followed by 56 pages on 'Topologies of Culture'. Steiner offers a fourfold division of what he calls the hermeneutic movement necessary to produce translation. First initiative, trust; then aggression ('the second move ... is incursive and extractive', which reminds me disagreeably of a visit to the dentist, though I suppose a sexual rather than a medical analogy is intended); then incorporation; and finally restitution. This somewhat scholastic classification does not seem to me particularly helpful; but it serves as a framework for the concrete treatment of actual examples, which after so much theorising brings life.

As an anatomist of translation Steiner has certain limitations. His main strength lies in his three chief languages. Dante is often quoted, but there is little handling of later Italian; there is no sign of direct acquaintance with Spanish, or Russian, or modern Greek.[4] Steiner does his best to deal with the problem of Chinese, but clearly lacks direct experience of the structural differences that separate this and other Oriental languages from the languages of Europe. He quotes Ezra Pound and Arthur Waley, and gives an appalling extract from a ponderous German rendering of Wang Wei by one Hans Bethge but not the new Wang Wei by Walter Robinson,[5] a scholar who can write poetry. He deals with several translations and imitations of Greek and Latin poems but without going deeply into the specific differences between these languages and those of modern Europe. Greek and Roman metre is fundamentally different from ours, since it depends on the quantities of vowels, not on stress, accent, or rhyme, and this means that many of its subtlest effects can hardly be indicated in translation. Here is a topic which I find more directly relevant to the central issue than much of the abstract theorising to which Steiner has devoted so much space.

But we must be grateful to Steiner for what he has given us, for it amounts to a good deal. His wide knowledge, acute intelligence and marked sensitivity to the nuances of poetical expression are everywhere in evidence. He deals entertainingly with travesties: with the sham Italian medievalism of Rossetti, with Littré's rendering of Dante into medieval French and Borchardt's rendering of him into

---

[4] Kimon Friar's magnificent translation of the *Odyssey* of Nikos Kazantzakis would supply an anatomist of translation with valuable material. Friar has described his intimate collaboration with Kazantzakis himself in the *Journal of Modern Literature*, vol. 11, no. 2 (1971-2), 215f.

[5] 1973.

medieval German. One of the best sections is devoted to the French struggle against Shakespeare. It reminds one of the price paid by French literature for its attainment of classic excellence during the seventeenth-century; it lost a quality which of the great writers of that time only La Fontaine knew how to keep. Mallarmé and his contemporaries worked desperately to recover it; Rimbaud intermittently succeeded. The late Dikran Garabedian, whose literal version of Shakespeare's sonnets into the French of Shakespeare's contemporaries[6] might interest Steiner, felt about French poetry after 1600 what Talleyrand felt about French life after 1789. Steiner is severe (as it seems to me, justly) about archaism in translation, which he thinks seldom comes off. I share his dislike for the sham Biblicism of Jowett's *Plato*; the valuable time lately devoted by a group of scholars under a learned editor to purging this work of its howlers might have been better spent on a replacement. I wonder what Steiner would say about the rendering of Herodotus into Biblical English by J. Enoch Powell. He admirably discusses two versions of Shakespeare's 87th sonnet by Stefan George and Karl Kraus. His analysis of several versions of a wonderful passage from the account of Priam's visit to Achilles in the last book of the *Iliad* lends substance to his judgment that though Pope's *Iliad* is a great poem in its own right no translation of this author gives more than a slight notion of the impact made by the original.

Steiner remarks that 'it is only lately that the translator – such as Constance Garnett, C.K. Scott Moncrieff, Arthur Waley – has been emerging from a background of indistinct servitude'. Anyone who knows what wages publishers pay to translators, and what miserable hacks they are consequently often forced to employ, will know the reason for this. Gifted writers whose bent lies towards translation are often treated little better than such hacks. Stephen MacKenna, whose wonderful translation of Plotinus he justly praises (and from whose journal he quotes some interesting remarks) almost starved in order to complete his work. Some major European writers cannot be properly appreciated by English readers unable to read them in the original, because good English translations do not exist. As for Constance Garnett, she does not deserve her place on Steiner's list. Years ago Sir Isaiah Berlin pointed out that she turned all the Russian authors whom she translated into the same grey, flat, muddy prose. No one reading Dostoevsky in her version would guess that he is often very funny; now that we have David Magarshack's translations, hers are no longer needed. Thomas Mann cannot possibly be appreciated by a

---

[6] *The Sonnets of Shakespeare translated into French 'regular' sonnets* (1964).

reader who knows him only in the ponderous and frequently inaccurate renderings of Mrs H.T. Lowe-Porter; not long ago a really good version of some of the short stories was published in America, but had to be withdrawn as a result of legal action. Some good translations of great writers are not as wholly satisfactory as they are thought to be. Scott Moncrieff's Proust is certainly far better than the continuation by Stanley Schiff; but when I have compared sections of it with the original I have been less impressed than I expected. His weakness is a tiresome kind of *New Statesman* competition cleverness, which is reflected in the catchpenny titles. How can he have rendered 'Aux Ombres des Jeunes Filles en Fleurs' by 'Within a Budding Grove', when Tennyson offered 'A Rosebud Garden of Girls'? But when Moncrieff was writing one was hardly allowed to mention Tennyson. Arthur Waley was a fine scholar as well as a remarkable writer, and his rendering of *The Tale of Genji* is a great achievement; but those competent to judge tell me that it has a thick patina of modernity.

The law of copyright ought not to limit people's right to offer new translations of books that deserve to be looked at from the point of view of more than one translator. Translators should be properly paid, but before being paid at all they should be carefully selected, for one small qualification they should have is an adequate knowledge of the language of the original. Corvo once agreed to meet a man called Sholto Douglas in a Brighton hotel and translate the Greek epigrammatist Meleager. When they got there, each found that the other knew no Greek, but this did not prevent the version from appearing. I have reviewed at least one translation by a translator no better qualified than they were.

The cause of translation will be greatly furthered by the existence of this learned and intelligent Anatomy, from whose study all readers, and not only intending translators, will greatly profit.

26

On Translations of Epic and Drama

By the 1960s Homeric translators had reached a point as far removed as possible from the romantic archaism of the classic Victorian versions. Even forty years before, these had begun to smell strongly of the classroom; their language made the subject-matter of the poems seem strangely remote from the life as it was now known. A fashion set in for versions in 'plain English', which renounced the attempt to convey a notion of the poetic character of Homer's writing. These versions have done valuable service. By their clarity, liveliness and lack of pomposity they have allowed the modern reader to enjoy the swift and exciting narrative of Homer, and have encouraged him to feel that the world of the epic is less remote from his own than he had at first supposed.

But the success of these versions has been won at a heavy price; and though their popularity has now reached its height, I will risk predicting that its days are numbered. Homer's language is nothing if not ornate, rich in resounding poetic compounds and gorgeous imagery; the belief of certain translators of the modern school that it must have stood close to the spoken language of its day can be shown to be absurd. The most obvious characteristics of the style and vocabulary of the poet are ones that translations of this sort utterly fail to bring out.

* Reviews of *The Anger of Achilles. Homer's Iliad* translated by Robert Graves in the *Listener*, 31 March 1960; *The Voyage of Argo* by Apollonius of Rhodes translated by E.V. Rieu in the *Spectator*, 6 February 1959; *The War at Troy: What Homer Didn't Tell* by F.M. Combellack in *CR* 19 (1969); *Essays in Antiquity* by Peter Green in *Time and Tide*, 17 December 1960; *Seven Against Thebes* translated by Anthony Hecht and Helen H. Bacon, *Antigone* translated by R.E. Braun, *Hippolytos* translated by Robert Bagg and *Iphigeneia in Tauris* translated by Richmond Lattimore in *The Times Literary Supplement*, 1 November 1974; *Aristophanes, Plays I and II* translated by Patric Dickinson in the *Spectator*, 2 January 1971. (The reviews of Robert Graves and E.V. Rieu were written many years ago. Nowadays I would write more politely about Apollonius, but not about Dr Rieu. Vian has now published the first volume of an excellent Budé *Apollonius*.)

Why have their authors chosen to present Homer in an idiom so radically different from his own? This happened because the whole character of modern life and literature had reached a point as far as possible from the atmosphere of the ancient epics. The modern reader had become wholly unsympathetic to the Homeric outlook; if he was to have Homer at all, he would have him only if reduced to his own measure. The exuberance of his language had to be pruned; and in place of the effects by which he had charmed his readers for three millénnia, his translators brought out qualities dear to the modern reader, but not hitherto observed in ancient writing. The Iliad was found to show subtle and exact psychological awareness; and the author (or authoress) of the Odyssey was found to have written a novel that had much in common with Jane Austen.

But there are grounds for suspecting that the modern world's remoteness from the ancient epic is now beginning to diminish. Even in England, poetry is beginning to show traces of its writers' awareness that we live in a violent and uncertain world, where there is little leisure to cultivate refined psychological perception in the manner of Virginia Woolf, and where at any moment the ancient heroic virtues may suddenly come to seem less meaningless than they did to Lytton Strachey. The time is approaching when the younger and livelier section of the reading public will demand a heroic and poetic rendering of Homer.[1]

Robert Graves's *The Anger of Achilles* is a version of the Iliad by one of the best English poets of our time; but it does not meet this need. Graves's kind of poetry is too different from Homer's; and he is typical of his generation in its approach to the ancient epic world. The greater part of the text is put into lucid, readable, colloquial, rather flat prose, not very different from the prose of Graves's novels. But every now and then there comes a snatch of verse, and these short poems are much the best thing in the book. None of them is in the least like Homer, and it would be unreasonable to expect from them the sustained height of lyric beauty of *Collected Poems, 1959*. Yet almost all bear witness to their author's exquisite ear and nervous, delicate use of language.

Wind, how fierce you blow,
  Clouds look dark as night,
Heavy flakes of snow
  Flutter from a height.

[1] E.g., since this essay was written, the versions of the Homeric poems by R. Lattimore and R. Fitzgerald.

The value of the book owes nothing to its introduction, in which many dubious or controversial statements are offered with excessive dogmatism. Graves implores Homer's pardon for the 'many small liberties' he has taken; Homer, he thinks, will grant his plea, 'despite protests from his loyal grammarians'. One grammarian, at least, thinks the liberties trivial by comparison with the book's main fault; Graves has left out all Homer's poetry. But he has given us some very pretty poems of his own; and some of us may doubt whether it is better to know Greek like Bentley than to write English verse like Graves.

The cover of E.V. Rieu's translation of Apollonius' *Voyage of the Argo* reproduces the Pistoxenus Painter's exquisite cylix showing Aphrodite riding on a bird. That bird is not a swan, as Dr Rieu supposes: it is a goose, and the choice of illustration is therefore apter than at first sight might be imagined. For Dr Rieu's attempt to show that Apollonius is more than a poet of the second rank does not convince. This writer had ingenuity, learning and great technical competence: yet he was in no way fit to be compared with his great contemporaries, Theocritus and Callimachus. True, it is unfair to judge Apollonius by the standard of the Homeric epic. He aimed to give pleasure by his dexterous command of the highly wrought poetical style which he affected, a style full of Homeric words and reminiscences, yet marked off from Homer's by its stricter metre, its closer texture and its careful avoidance of the literal reproduction of Homeric idiom. He was a learned poet writing for a learned audience, who would delight in their ability to trace his sometimes recondite allusions. Like most of his contemporaries, he excelled in the depiction of scenes from daily life and in the description of amorous passion; so that he is at his best in the comparisons with everyday scenes which, after Homer's model, he makes frequent use of, and in his famous account of Medea's love for Jason. With the epic and the heroic he, like the other Alexandrians, had little real sympathy: only, unlike most of the others, he was not wise enough to realise it. But even on his strongest ground he falls well below the best of his contemporaries – only compare the best Apollonian similes with Callimachus' account of the storm coming over a clear sky and of the early dawn near Marathon, or the Apollonian Medea with Simaetha in the first idyll of Theocritus. Theocritus and Callimachus, like all the best Greek poetry, are easy to learn by heart: Apollonius is practically impossible.

Dr Rieu in his introduction makes a brave attempt to get round these awkward facts. The ground is made easier for him by his omission to describe the style of the original poem or the effects its author intended to create, so that he is free to invest it with 'romantic' character and to give its writer credit for various desirable attributes, such as a 'deep understanding of human nature' and a 'quiet sense of humour' which no one who has tried to read him in his proper context would agree were there. Dr Rieu tries to excuse the intolerable colourlessness of the Apollonian Jason on the ground that the poet has not set out to portray a hero, but an 'ordinary man'. This defence is unconvincing; especially since every other character except Medea is as dull as Jason. Even for Medea, Dr Rieu claims too much. The lovesick girl of Book III is a different person from the formidable sorceress of Book IV; and the former is as much inferior to Theocritus' Simaetha as is the latter to the Medea of Euripides.

Our chief reason for being grateful for the survival of the *Argonautica* is that we are able to appreciate the skill with which Virgil has adapted his many borrowings from Apollonius. Yet this lightly wrought, artificial and learned work is not without a characteristic charm; and it is a pity that Dr Rieu has made no effort to convey it. The style of the *Argonautica* is rich, ornate, highly coloured, nothing if not poetical: Dr Rieu renders it in an easy, fluent, readable, flat and Isabella-coloured prose. He maintains a very fair (though not an impeccable) level of accuracy: and he shows considerable dexterity in transmuting the immensely different idiom of the original into his own. Yet just as his introduction utterly fails to explain the spirit and the purpose of the poet, so his translation gives no notion whatever of the impression given by the language and the style of the original. Dr Rieu's version is commendably free from the irritating sort of 'tushery' that marks so many archaising translations of Greek literature. But it includes a number of no less irritating modernisms. Medea and her sister refer to Aeetes as 'Father', so that we think of corresponding scenes in Wimpole Street: the Amazons were 'by no means gentle, well-conducted folk': and so on.

Dr Rieu's translations of Homer have had a phenomenal success: and it is likely that this book, too, will be successful, probably far more so than would a translation that more faithfully reproduced the character of the original. Those who know the originals may at first be puzzled by the popularity of these clear and readable, but flat and pedestrian versions of the ancient epics. But their success is not surprising. The preoccupation of serious novelists with psychological niceties, which only now shows signs of being relaxed, has starved the modern public of the pleasure that every reader gets from a good plot. These renderings allow him to enjoy a good plot without subjecting him to the torture which he with his restricted leisure and his utilitarian bias finds the cruellest of all – that of having to struggle with a style which is intricate enough to make some demand on his alertness or ornate enough to make some demand on his aesthetic faculty. Still we should be grateful to Dr Rieu for what he has done to make ancient epic popular, even while we recognise that he owes much of his success to the same factors that account for the fashion for detective stories.

A brief glossary at the end of the present book explains the more important persons and places, but readers are given less help in understanding the numerous mythological allusions than they might reasonably expect. Some will be interested, though perhaps also disappointed, to learn that the legend that Phrixus's ram *flew* to Colchis is almost certainly later than Apollonius: Professor Donald Robertson has shown that according to all the best authorities he *swam*.

Among the late Greek epic poets Quintus is by far the worst. Nonnus, tasteless and turgid beyond measure as he is throughout the immense length of the *Dionysiaca* and the *Paraphrase*, has a ghastly vitality that carries the reader – or at least some readers – along with him. But the anaemic pastiche served up by Quintus is utterly devoid of life; even the Oenone episode in the tenth book is good only by comparison with what surrounds it. Not surprisingly, the only English version so far is the rendering into Victorian traditionalist verse by a kindred spirit, A.S. Way, whose *Euripides* the Loeb Library ought to stop reprinting.

In his new prose translation, Mr Combellack has aimed (p. 21) to be clear and faithful to the original, and he has achieved these aims. In a rendering of Quintus it is impossible to avoid archaisms, since the original consists of nothing else, and if some of the archaisms in this work are irritating, so are those of Quintus. More often the author fails through timid modernising, like that of the new English translation of the New Testament ('because he was an especially intimate friend', 'carefully hiding their sex organs, as is proper') or through clumsy literalism ('he was just like one who is groaning', 'for, truly great grief increases with good women, when their husbands are dead'). Still, it is not much more distasteful than the original, and it maintains a very fair level of accuracy. The introduction offers neither adequate information nor acute criticism, and the footnotes are neither numerous nor particularly helpful. To complain that Andromache at the moment of her grief is said to have slender ankles shows little understanding of the nature of the conventional epithet, and to complain that Homer calls both Laodice and Cassandra the loveliest of Priam's daughters shows little understanding of how the

Mediterranean peoples to this day employ superlatives.

A public that will buy a million copies of Rieu's *Odyssey* presumably reads epic for the plot, and any reader knowing only English who wishes to read Quintus will be adequately served by this translation.[2]

In a most interesting essay Peter Green presents the reflections induced in him by an examination of all the English versions of the *Agamemnon* he could lay his hands on.[3] Until very recent times, nearly all of these are either word-for-word renderings with no literary character at all or else specimens, whether good or bad, of some particular type of English poem that do little or nothing to give the reader any notion of the kind of impact made by the style and idiom of the original. Dr Green argues that the kind of free verse that has come to dominate English poetry during the last thirty years offers an excellent opportunity to those eager to produce the sort of version that, while having a real poetic character of its own, tries to affect the reader in a way as like as possible to that of the original.

This essay seems to me to be a very valuable piece of work. Let us hope that its appearance indicates that we are soon to be delivered from those renderings of Greek poetry into clear, readable, flat, matter-of-fact prose which make so little demand upon the reader's attention that tired business men in trains find them as relaxing as a detective story. Apart from having exciting plots, the *Iliad* and the *Odyssey* happened to be written in poetry; a fact that is scarcely to be guessed by the reader who knows them only from the most popular modern English translation. The *Agamemnon* that Green singles out for praise is that of Louis MacNeice; and it is certainly better verse and a better version than any of its modern competitors. (Yet can one feel quite sure that it, or any other version of its kind, will seem as acceptable in thirty years time as it does now?)

---

[2] Those who know French will prefer the accurate and spirited rendering that accompanies the excellent Budé edition of Francis Vian, whose first two volumes have been reviewed in *CR* lxxix (1964), 257f. and lxxxii (1967), 275f., and whose third and last volume is expected shortly. Those who want a good general account of Quintus will not turn to Combellack's introduction but to the concise and learned article of Rudolf Keydell in *R.-E.* xxiv (1963), 1271f. Combellack has translated the old Teubner text of Zimmermann; his version was made, he tells us, before Vian's first volume reached him, and his work shows no sign of acquaintance with Keydell. He would have been wise to wait until he was able to make full use of both these important contributions to the study of his author.

[3] *Essays in Antiquity* (1960); see also R.A. Brower, 'Seven Agamemnons' in *On Translation* (Harv. Studies in Comp. Lit. 1959), 173-95.

No modern English poetical version of a Greek tragedy, except Louis MacNeice's *Agamemnon*, can compete with the best American attempts. Modern verse forms are in many ways better fitted than older ones to deal with the special difficulties presented by Greek poetry, and no one has taken better advantage of this fact than Richmond Lattimore. The Chicago series of translations of Greek drama contains some excellent specimens of his art; but it also contains pieces by others that are less successful, and the Prentice Hall series offers close renderings with few literary pretensions. The aim of the new Oxford series, we are told on the jacket, is 'to recreate the entire corpus of Greek tragedy as though it had been written originally in the English language of our time'. The main difficulty in the way of this plan is that it wasn't, and could not have been. But all the translators of the four plays now published are aware of this; and such an attitude is greatly preferable to that which sees Greek tragedy as something infinitely remote. The proof of the pudding is in the eating, and each of these versions has merit, two of them in large measure.

'The translators,' we are told, 'are all poets, some are classical scholars as well, and those who are not have collaborated with well-known scholars.' This reminds one of Bernard Shaw's reply to Mrs Patrick Campbell's suggestion that they should have a child which would inherit her beauty and his brains; but the only volume among these four which is the product of collaboration happens to be most successful. In rendering the *Seven Against Thebes*, Anthony Hecht, one of the best American poets now writing, has been assisted by a reliable scholar in Helen Bacon. They rightly maintain that this play, the third and sole survivor of a trilogy, is a great work, and they have produced a version well calculated to make this clear to those who read it.

Renouncing the attempt at exact reproduction of the effect of the original, Hecht breaks up the iambic trimeters of dialogue into irregular shorter lines of free verse, and since similar lines are used to render lyrics the Greekless reader will not easily perceive, as he will when reading Lattimore's *Iphigeneia*, which parts were sung in the original and which spoken. The style of the original is a grand style, and this is not; in places it descends to the colloquial in a manner very unlike Aeschylus. There is a good deal of expansion, not all of which is justified. Yet the directness of Aeschylus comes across, and so does the element of roughness that is inseparable from his strength. One gets the impression that Miss Bacon has faithfully fulfilled her task of interpreting the sense of the original, and that when Hecht departs from it he does so consciously and in obedience to his own poetic instinct. He cannot be blamed for this; but the Greekless reader should be warned that he cannot rely on this version as a mirror of the original in the same way as he can rely on one by Lattimore. Hecht's version shows an excellent sense of the dramatic, and the action on the stage is everywhere envisaged; in particular the great scene in which the messenger describes the seven champions advancing against the seven gates and the king in reply describes the seven champions whom he sends against them is powerfully and truly rendered. This translation should be most effective in production.

Richard Emil Braun in his *Antigone* and Robert Bagg in his *Hippolytus* adopt a method more akin to that of Hecht than to that of Lattimore. Neither of them is as successful as Hecht, but neither is without success. Although Braun is a professional classical scholar and Bagg is not, the former gets the meaning wrong more often than the latter. Bagg had the advantage of being able to use one of the finest commentaries on a Greek play, that which W.S. Barrett published only nine years ago. Sophocles is a very difficult author, and Braun has relied almost entirely on R.C. Jebb. Jebb's is still by far the most useful commentary, and he had far better taste than most scholars; but the work of the past few years has not been entirely fruitless, and Braun might have done more to profit by it. But to compensate for this defect he has a genuine poetic gift; a man who can render the words of Ismene that means literally 'Your heart is warm over things that are cold' by 'This ardor of yours is spent on ashes' can be forgiven a few mistakes of fact. Bagg, a professor of English who is known as a poet, is more accurate but less poetical; but he has added to the value of his book by the good sense shown in his introduction. He sees the play not as some learned readers will see it, as a cautionary tale in which Hippolytus is 'punished' for his pride, but as a tragedy, in which the hero risks all and loses all for the sake of a relationship with Artemis that for him is worth the risk.

I have left the old master till last. William Arrowsmith, the general editor, rightly says that Lattimore's talents are particularly suited to the *Iphigeneia in Tauris*. This play and the *Helen*, which is so like it, are not great masterpieces in the same sense as the other three now published. But they possess a rare and magic quality; the work in English which gives the best notion of their character is *The Tempest*. The difference that separates these plays from tragedies cannot be brought out by saying that they are comedies; although they end happily, the ending is in doubt till late in the action, and a melancholy light is cast over the play from the beginning by sad events that have happened far away or long ago. The lyrics are not great poetry on the plane of Aeschylus and Sophocles; they have much of the quality of a libretto. But a Metastasio does not merit contempt, and the lyrics of these plays serve to convey an atmosphere of calm resignation and autumnal beauty. No reader has responded more to their peculiar charm than Goethe and, if they had not existed, neither *Iphigenie* nor the second part of *Faust* would be the same.

This special quality of the *Iphigeneia* is most successfully communicated by the refined simplicity and delicate exactitude of what seems to me one of the very best of Lattimore's translations. In Arrowsmith's words, he is able to produce a version of a Greek play which is 'not only remarkably faithful but poetry of a high order'. His longer dialogue line is less unlike the Greek trimeter than the shorter lines favoured by the other translators. He is scrupulous to render so far as possible the exact sense of the original; and here he has the special advantage of being a scholar of the first quality. But hardly any other scholar could have achieved the smooth and polished texture of a verse perfectly adapted to the special quality of the poetry that is being rendered.

Different as they are from one another, the versions of Hecht and Lattimore are marked off from the others by the sureness of their taste. Lattimore never distresses the reader by an alarming lapse. Hecht does so once only, when he gratuitously drags in the hideous expression 'menstrual pulse', though there are other places where he indulges unnecessarily in the sexual imagery so loved by our Freud-ridden age. Yet one cannot imagine either of them allowing Creon to address the prophet as 'Dear old Tiresias' or calling Hippolytus' mother a 'bareback Amazon queen' and so dragging in an irrelevant reminiscence of Adah Menken; still less turning a cult-song to Artemis into a personal romantic tribute or missing the relevance of the great ode about human achievements in the *Antigone* through not realising that the key word of it means 'formidable'.[4]

The reactions of successive ages to Aristophanes make a fascinating study, and they have supplied the subject of an extremely intelligent and amusing German book, *Aristophanes in der Nachwelt*, by Wilhelm Süss. In our time, now that class and race have replaced sex as the main targets of the moral indignation of the *bien pensant*, the incentive to translate this poet is powerful. Until quite lately, most English people read him in the nineteenth-century version of the barrister Benjamin Bickley Rogers, whose poetic manner derives from that of

---

[4] On such distinctions, see also M.R. Lefkowitz, 'Cultural conventions and the persistence of mistranslations', *CJ* 68 (1972), 31-8.

W.S. Gilbert – also a strong influence, hardly less than Swinburne, on the style of Gilbert Murray, his cousin, who was named after him. In its way Rogers's translation is a remarkable *tour de force*; but it presents the poet through spectacles somewhat like those of Dickens's benevolent old gentlemen and its bowdlerising tendency suppresses an essential element of the original.

More than half the eleven plays are now available in lively American versions published by the University of Michigan Press – an excellent *Frogs* by Richmond Lattimore, other plays by William Arrowsmith and Douglass Parker – and we are now offered a two-volume edition of all of them, translated by Patric Dickinson.

A well-known cockney comic, who had acted in several Greek comedies on the radio, once told me that he much preferred Menander to Aristophanes; the jokes, he said, were of the kind he had heard all his life. So are many of the jokes in Aristophanes; but I think my friend was confused by the numerous allusions of the Old Comedy to facts and persons known to all at the time of first production but nowadays obscure. Fifth-century Athens was so small that the comic poet could use a well-known character to raise a laugh as easily as the writer of a school play; and much of his subject-matter came from political or social situations peculiar to that time and place.

This presents a translator with a problem. If he sets out to explain the allusions in footnotes, he risks swamping his reader with unwanted detail: if he leaves them unexplained, the reader may complain that part of the play is unintelligible. The Michigan editors give a short introduction to each play and short explanatory notes printed after it: Dickinson supplements his short introductions with nothing but a 'glossary and index of names' which gives the briefest possible explanations. Some may think this is too little. But Dickinson clearly wants the reader to read fast and to enjoy the play without being plagued with too much historical detail, and there is much to be said for his point of view.

Do the allusions make the plays obscure and disagreeable matter for the modern reader? If he reads a good version, as this certainly is, they do not. Apart from the aid the translator has provided, much of what we need to know is made clear by the play itself. Detailed knowledge of Greek history and society certainly add to the reader's enjoyment: but Aristophanes has much to offer even to the reader who approaches him in a state of utter ignorance.

Menander's comedies have a structure which resembles that of many modern comedies. These plays are quite different. The plot, in so far as they have one, is usually a fantasy with a strong element of wish-fulfilment: the hero, most often an ordinary middle-aged

Athenian like a typical member of the audience, is able by a show of common sense and resolution combined with supernatural good luck to triumph over the familiar limits to human satisfaction – war, limited means, politicians, the unavailability of pretty girls.

In *The Birds*, which is perhaps the most brilliant of the plays – it had immense success when acted here in modern Greek by the Athenian Theatre Royal – the hero joins the birds in founding an ideal city in the clouds, and puts pressure on the gods by cutting off their food supply: in the last play, *Ploutos*, the hero finds the blind god of wealth, takes him to the healing god's temple to restore his sight, and makes him enrich, for once, only deserving people like himself. Four plays are mainly concerned with the long war against Sparta and her allies which Athens was fighting during their production. Aristophanes adopts the standpoint of the conservative farmers of some means who loathed the war because it caused them hardships; he is against the demagogues and the city mob who favoured war. That seems to have been the viewpoint, to judge from most inadequate remains, of the other comic poets of the time also. Were they seriously crusading to stop the war, as many moderns have assumed? Or did they simply find this point of view both congenial to a great part of their audience and convenient for their mixture of fantasy and satire? Certainly Aristophanes came into conflict with the radical politician Cleon, a strong supporter of the war; Cleon prosecuted him for an attack on himself made in the now lost *Babylonians*, and the extant *Knights* is entirely devoted to ridiculing him. But was the poet's motive purely political? Did he really write to persuade people to withdraw support from Cleon, or did he simply find that Cleon provided good material for traditional comic treatment?

The same problem arises with other butts of Aristophanes, like Socrates and Euripides. Taken at face value, Aristophanes' words imply that he thought these persons, like other famous intellectuals of the time, were dangerous corrupters of public morals. Yet Plato in his *Symposium* represents Aristophanes and Socrates as being on friendly terms, and it is highly doubtful whether the portrayal of Socrates in the *Clouds* is more than a caricature. So, for the most part, is Aristophanes' portrait of Euripides, a writer with whose plays and music he was beyond doubt intimately familiar. In a free society intellectuals, like politicians, normally provide comedy with much of its subject-matter: whether the comic poet seriously disapproves of them and wishes to undermine their position with the public is another matter. One need not be an enemy of existentialism to make fun of Sartre or Beckett, nor an enemy of socialism to see that there are comic possibilities in Lord George-Brown.

The *Lysistrata*, perhaps the best-known play of Aristophanes has led some people to take him seriously as a feminist. But compare it with *The Assembly of Women*, in which the women of Athens put on false beards and take over the assembly and the government, and you see that for this author the whole idea of women taking any such initiative was wildly funny simply because in his society it was so utterly out of the question.

Aristophanes is, among other things, a valuable source of information about Greek history and Greek society. But the moment you forget he is a poet and treat him as a repository of historical facts, the moment you forget he is writing comedy and start to take him altogether seriously, you are in danger.

In the Greek, the actual words of these plays have unbelievable charm. There are many scenes of wild farce, made particularly delightful by a zestful and innocent indecency of a kind which no one who has known only a society which is or has been Christian is likely to have encountered in real life.

Some of the dialogue is not far distant, it would seem, from the language used in life, but often there are huge compound words and vast rhetorical amplifications; very often there is skilful parody of the language and manner of high poetry. There is much lyric poetry of the greatest beauty, and with an astonishingly wide range; some of the lyrics are written in a style far simpler than that of the lyric verse of tragedy.

No classical Greek poet is easy to translate, and this one is exceptionally difficult. Mr Dickinson is modest about his Greek. It is not bad, although he might have made more effort to employ the aids which are available. That his version is not suitable for use as a crib is wholly to his credit; yet sometimes he misses a nuance that makes a slight difference to the sense or to the poetry. On the whole the Michigan translators have more vigour, but Mr Dickinson has a better ear, and his version has a smoother and more polished texture. Offered at a fairly low price and in a most attractive format, his work deserves, and is likely to have, considerable success.

27

Tacitus

Like several earlier historians of Rome, Tacitus had a distinguished career in the service of the Roman state. Cornelius Tacitus – whether his first name was Gaius or Publius is uncertain – was born in 56 or 57 AD, when Claudius had been Emperor for five years. At about this time a certain Cornelius Tacitus held the not unimportant post of financial agent of the government in Gallia Belgica, and he may have been the father of the great historian. Definite evidence is lacking, but it is likely that Tacitus was one of the many distinguished Romans of the time to come from a provincial family. Several facts seem to indicate that the place of his origin was Gallia Narbonensis, the southern strip of France, which had been acquired by Rome long before Caesar's conquest of the main part of Gaul. But by the time of the historian's adolescence, his family must have moved to Rome.

As a young man Tacitus received the elaborate training in oratory that was necessary for all who aspired to high office in the Roman state. We learn something of his early years from his *Dialogue on Orators*, a work of uncertain date but perhaps published in 102 AD, when the friend to whom it is dedicated held the consulship. The dialogue is supposed to take place during Vespasian's reign, in 75; and among its characters are two of the leading orators of that time, to whom Tacitus, according to the usual Roman custom, attached himself to serve a kind of apprenticeship. The subject of the work is one much discussed at that time – the decline of Roman eloquence. It reveals a dissatisfaction with the superficial training in declamation on imaginary and sometimes ridiculous subjects with which many of Tacitus' contemporaries were content, and expounds the same exalted conception of the orator that had been held by Cicero and was revived by the leading teacher of rhetoric in Tacitus' own time, Quintilian. Poetry, history, and philosophy must be studied by the aspiring orator; he should learn his trade not by performing artificial

* Introduction to *Tacitus, The Annals and the Histories* (Great History Series, edited by H.R. Trevor-Roper 1964; 1978).

exercises under a professional teacher, but by attaching himself to some eminent advocate and politician whom he can accompany to the scenes of his activity and observe in action. Tacitus was to become the leading orator of his time, and must have distinguished himself from the first in this capacity.

At about the age of twenty, an aspirant for office like the young Tacitus would normally serve for a year with a legion as military tribune. Tacitus may have done this in 76 or 77. In the latter year he was betrothed to the daughter of one of the most eminent Romans of the time, Cnaeus Julius Agricola. Agricola's father originated from Forum Julii (now Fréjus) in Gallia Narbonensis (Narbonese Gaul), and had reached the praetorship. As a young man Agricola took part in the suppression of Boudicca's revolt in Britain, and after holding the praetorship he commanded a legion there. Under Vespasian he successfully governed Aquitania, in Gaul, and during the year of his daughter's betrothal he held the consulship. At its conclusion he became governor of Britain, where he remained for seven years. Agricola's model governorship was marked both by military victories and by notable success in promoting civilisation among the Britons; but it was rewarded by no further promotion. The Emperor Domitian looked on him with fear and jealousy, and when the time came at which Agricola might have taken part in the ballot for the two most coveted provinces, Africa and Asia, he was advised not to compete. This neglect did not provoke Agricola to any show of dissatisfaction; and when he died at the early age of fifty-three he had been prudent enough to name the Emperor among his heirs.

Passing through the normal stages of the official career, Tacitus was probably quaestor in 81 or 82, and then aedile or military tribune two or three years later. In 88 he held the office of praetor, and was also accorded an important priesthood, being made one of the fifteen members of the priestly college concerned with the administration of the secular games held in that year (see *Annals* XI, 11). After his praetorship he left for an appointment in the provinces, and when his father-in-law died in 93 he had been out of Rome for four years. For the last year of this period he may have been governor of a minor province.

Tacitus held the consulship during part of the year 97, the year after Domitian's murder and the succession of the admirable Nerva. It is not safe to guess that he owed his consulship to the change of emperor. Instances are not wanting of consuls, who had been designated in advance, holding the office even after the death of the emperor by whom they had been chosen and the official condemnation of his memory; and the succession of offices held by

Tacitus under Domitian shows that the hatred for that Emperor's tyranny which he revealed after Domitian's death found no open expression while he was alive. As consul he pronounced with dignity and eloquence the funeral oration of the eminent Verginius Rufus, three times consul, who after Nero's death in 68 had refused the offer of his troops to make him emperor. Three years later, under Trajan, Tacitus joined another famous writer, his friend the younger Pliny, in prosecuting a former governor of Africa, Marius Priscus, on charges of extortion and oppression. Priscus was condemned and exiled, though as Juvenal comments dryly, the unfortunate provincials were no better off for that. Doubtless Tacitus held other offices, probably abroad; and we know from an inscription that in 112-13 he held the appointment that above all others set the seal on a distinguished public career – the proconsulate of Asia. How long he survived after that is not certain; but it seems likely that he lived some years into the reign of Hadrian.

The works of Tacitus

The earliest of Tacitus' works was probably the short biography of his father-in-law, Agricola, which seems to have been published either not long before or not long after the death of Nerva and the accession of Trajan, on 28 January, 98 AD. The panegyric on a famous man was at this time an accepted literary genre; so was the historical excursus on a particular country or a particular campaign; and the *Agricola* is something between the two. Soon afterwards, perhaps in 99, while the new Emperor was still absent on the Rhine, Tacitus published the *Germania*, a monograph on the country and people of Germany. The subject could not have been more topical, nor the treatment more acceptable to authority; for the warning against the danger to Rome presented by the Germans must have been welcome to an emperor then actively engaged in guarding against this threat. Much of the information in the book was already out of date at the time of publication; no doubt it came from written sources. The author characteristically contrasts the primitive virtues of the barbarians with the civilised vices of his countrymen. In modern times the work has supplied material to believers in the noble savage and to writers on the German character, for and against.

   Although the *Histories* begin where the *Annals*, when complete, finished, they were written earlier. Part of them seems to have circulated in 105, and in 106 Tacitus asked his friend Pliny for information about the eruption of Vesuvius in 79, in which his uncle, the elder Pliny, had lost his life. The *Histories* begin with the first day of 69 AD, the Year of the Four Emperors. They were in twelve books. Only the first four books and the first twenty-six chapters of Book V are extant. Book I describes the murder of Galba, the accession of Otho, and the march of Vitellius' armies from Germany across the Alps. Book II contains the war between Otho and Vitellius, Otho's suicide, and the proclamation of Vespasian as emperor by the eastern armies. Book III begins with Antonius Primus' invasion of Italy and describes the defeat of Vitellius' generals at Cremona, the burning of the Capitol, the occupation of Rome, and the death of Vitellius. Book IV is mainly occupied with the revolt of the Batavi under Julius Civilis which followed the march from Germany of Vitellius' legions. The surviving fragment of Book V begins with Titus' siege of Jerusalem and finishes off with Civilis' rebellion. The book probably contained the whole story of the siege, and may have gone on well into Vespasian's reign, perhaps as far as 73 AD. Book VI probably ended with the death of Vespasian in 79; if so, Books VII-XII will have contained the fifteen years of Domitian's reign.

Tacitus probably went straight on to write the *Annals*, which were in eighteen books. Book II, Chapter 61 can hardly have been written after 117 AD; that is the most positive indication we have of the date of the work's composition. Book I begins with the death of Augustus and the accession of Tiberius in 14 AD. The first six books contained Tiberius' reign and ended with his death; but our single manuscript breaks off soon after the beginning of Book V, just before the imprisonment of Germanicus' widow and her elder son. All the rest of Book V and some thirty chapters of Book VI are missing; the narrative starts again just after the execution of Sejanus. Books VII-XII covered the reigns of Gaius and Claudius; but Books VII-X are entirely lost, and only about half (the second half) of Book XI survives. What we have of Book XI describes the final episodes in the career of Messallina, and Book XII carries the narrative to the death of Claudius. Books XIII-XVIII were devoted to the reign of Nero; but about halfway through Book XVI the manuscript finally breaks off.

Tacitus in later times

The younger Pliny predicted that his friend's historical works would be immortal; but they rapidly went out of fashion in the archaising and mannered second century; nor did the rise of Christianity, of which Tacitus speaks so scathingly, assist his reputation to recover. But in 275 the Emperor Tacitus, who claimed to be a descendant of the historian, took measures to ensure the survival of his works; and during the fourth century they seem to have enjoyed some esteem. They influenced several writers of imperial biography at that time; and Ammianus Marcellinus, a Greek of Antioch, continued Tacitus' *Histories* from the death of Nerva down to the death of the Emperor Valens in 378, in a Latin history which is not unworthy of its model. During the fifth century, an age of disaster for the Empire, Tacitus could still be censured by the Christian historian Orosius and praised by the poet Sidonius Apollinaris. But with the eclipse of polite letters his works must have been scarce; for in the sixth century we find the learned Cassiodorus referring to him as 'a certain Cornelius'.

During the dark centuries that follow, we hear nothing of Tacitus. Petrarch, surprisingly, says nothing of him. The first humanist to show acquaintance with his writings is Boccaccio, who seems to have acquired his knowledge about 1370. During the fifteenth century several writers show a knowledge of his work (except the first six books of the *Annals*). But these early humanists were too intoxicated with Cicero to relish an author who systematically rejected the Ciceronian symmetry in sentence construction; and they were too obsessed with style to value Tacitus for his content.

The first printed text of Tacitus was published by John of Spires at Venice in 1470. It contained *Annals* XI-XVI and all that survives of the *Histories*, together with the three minor works. What was published of the *Annals* and the *Histories* had been preserved by a single manuscript copied at Monte Cassino during the eleventh century; the minor works had survived in a manuscript at Hersfeld in Germany. The former is now at Florence and is known as Codex Mediceus II; the latter disappeared, and has had to be reconstructed laboriously from a number of descendants. Early in the present century part of it was discovered in the library of an Italian nobleman; the owner obstinately refused to allow scholars to make use of it until 1939, when a learned German achieved access, using the powerful persuasion of Heinrich Himmler, to whom he later dedicated his edition. *Annals* I-VI also survived the Middle Ages in a single manuscript, copied at Corvey in Germany during the ninth century, and first edited by the younger Beroaldus under the auspices of the cultivated Pope Leo X (Giovanni de' Medici) in 1515. It is known as Codex Mediceus I, and is also in Florence.

One might have expected that Niccolò Machiavelli would recognise Tacitus as a kindred spirit; and in fact he quotes him more often and with more approval than any previous writer since the printing of his works. But Tacitus meant less to Machiavelli than did Livy, and his main political work, the *Discorsi*, centres on the discussion of Livy and not of Tacitus. Had Machiavelli known the first six books of the *Annals* he might have reacted differently; but he wrote *The Prince* two years before and the *Discorsi* only a year after their first printing. In the *Discorsi* he does not quote them, and it is not likely that he had read them when he wrote it. Livy, whose style is so much more like that of Cicero, was at that time much the more famous author; and Livy's history dealt with a time when Rome was a republic, as Florence was for most of Machiavelli's lifetime.

Yet in the second half of the sixteenth century Tacitus was to acquire astonishing popularity. A reaction against Ciceronianism made it easier to appreciate his style. As early as 1532, Beatus Rhenanus, the friend and biographer of Erasmus, proclaimed Tacitus superior to Livy. But Tacitus did not owe his rise to favour to his style alone. Humanists were becoming less interested in style and more in content; and with the rise of absolute monarchies all over Europe, his content acquired a special interest. Although Machiavelli had failed to champion Tacitus in the way we might have expected, Tacitus owed no small part of the fame he enjoyed during the sixteenth and seventeenth centuries to the Florentine. For at the time of the Council of Trent, the Pope placed Machiavelli on the Index. He could not safely be discussed; but what was to hinder writers interested in political theory from commenting upon the work of a long dead classical historian, a work well calculated to promote the discussion of many burning topics of the age? Scholarly guidance was given to these 'Tacitisti' by the great humanist of the Low Countries Justus Lipsius, whose commentary first appeared in 1574, to be followed seven years later by his first edition of the text. Soon afterward Charles Paschal in France, Annibale Scoti in Italy, and Alamos de Barrientes in Spain wrote political commentaries on Tacitus. From this time until the end of the seventeenth century Tacitus served as a peg on which to hang all kinds of political discussion. There flowed from the presses of France, Italy, Spain, Germany, and Holland a stream of collections of aphorisms, treatises, and 'discourses' in the Machiavellian manner that used Tacitus as a pretext for the airing of all kinds of contemporary issues. These writers adopted the most diverse attitudes toward their chosen author. In the conflicts between Christianity and *Realpolitik*, between kingship and liberty, both sides might claim him as an ally and both sides might denounce him as an enemy. The learned Lipsius made out Tacitus almost as a Christian; the acute Jesuit Firmiano Strada attacked him as a Machiavellian. To Scipione Ammirato and Filippo Cavriana, who dedicated their works on Tacitus to the Grand Duke of Tuscany, Tacitus was the friend of kings; to Bacon he was the enemy of tyrants. Bacon's view was shared by the most distinguished of the 'Tacitisti,' Traiano Boccalini, who in a book published at about the time of his death, in 1613, amusingly describes how the author of a panegyric on the present age is cured by Apollo, who makes him the present of a pair of Tacitean spectacles. Boccalini's own *Observations on Tacitus* remained unpublished until 1677. The Senate of Venice referred a request for permission to print them to a commission of five senators, who reported that it was Tacitus' teaching that had produced Machiavelli 'and other evil authors.'

We must not imagine that at this time Tacitus was valued only as a substitute for Machiavelli. Many read and esteemed him for his own sake. His influence may be seen in the work of every important French moralist from Montaigne to La Rochefoucauld; and the most splendid literary monument to Tacitus, eclipsing Ben Jonson's *Sejanus* (1603), Corneille's *Othon* (1665), and Alfieri's *Ottavia* (1780), is Racine's *Britannicus* (1669).

England was less concerned with Tacitus than the Continent during the sixteenth and seventeenth centuries, perhaps because of the singularity of its political development. But in 1622 a Dutch refugee, Isaac Dorislaus, who had begun to lecture on the *Annals* at Cambridge, was stopped before he had got to the end of the first chapter. Four years later Sir John Eliot in the House of Commons enraged Charles I by comparing Strafford to Sejanus; and in 1657 Piero Negesch, who had lived in England, published in his native Italian a comparison between Tiberius and Cromwell, much to the advantage of the former. The first important English writer on Tacitus, Thomas Gordon (1684-1750), true to the native empiricism, pours scorn on the dull commonplaces and lifeless paraphrases which he finds typical of the 'Tacitists'. Not that his own commentary is closer than theirs to its ostensible subject; it is a political pamphlet against monarchy.

Tacitus was considered an apostle of liberty by a number of eighteenth-century writers: Rousseau, d'Alembert, and Diderot saw him in this light. He was a hero to the apologists of the French Revolution, especially to Camille Desmoulins; and not surprisingly Napoleon pursued him with a deadly hatred. The Emperor planned to write a commentary to refute Tacitus, attacked him in two articles in the *Journal des Débats*, and wanted to have him removed from the syllabus at the Ecole Normale.

> *Tacite en train de flamme accuse nos Séjans*
> *Et son nom prononcé fait pâlir les tyrans*

wrote Joseph-Marie Chénier. The lines cost him his post as an inspector of schools.

Tacitus profoundly influenced Vico and Montesquieu, who both understood him far better than most of their predecessors and contemporaries; but in general the eighteenth century admired him less than the preceding age. To a severe classicism his style is uncongenial; and to doubts about his style were added doubts about his matter. Fénelon and Bayle had both made reservations with regard to Tacitus, and Voltaire looked upon him with a cold eye. To him Tacitus seemed '*un fanatique pétillant d'esprit*'; he found it hard to believe in the excesses of Tiberius on Capri or the atrocities of Nero. '*Je conçois,*' he wrote, '*que tout Romain avait l'âme républicain dans son cabinet, et que Tacite se venge quelque fois, la plume à la main, sur l'usurpation de l'empereur.*' But if Tacitus was not greatly admired by those eighteenth-century writers who did most to win for the period its title of the Age of Reason, a notable exception is Edward Gibbon. Gibbon explicitly refuted Voltaire's arguments against Tacitus, for whom he expressed the greatest admiration. 'I know of no one except Tacitus,' he once wrote, 'who has quite come up to my ideas of a philosophic historian.'[1]

The rise of new historical methods together with the vast increase in the amount of detailed study of the past caused Tacitus to be subjected to a detailed scrutiny during the nineteenth century. The period covered by his writings has been the subject of minute researches; his handling of his sources and his credibility as a witness have been carefully examined; he has become the centre of a vast literature. Judged by the canons of historical method that came into vogue during the century of Burckhardt, Ranke, and Mommsen, Tacitus must appear deficient. From nineteenth-century Germany came much adverse criticism of a historian whose methods outraged its scholarly requirements and whose attitude contrasted lamentably with its cherished principle of trust in rulers. Ranke offered a fair and balanced judgment, but even his admiration is mixed with disapproval; and at the close of the century Friedrich Leo tried to excuse Tacitus' deficiencies on the ground that he was no historian, but a poet.

In our own time the climate of opinion has become more favourable to Tacitus. One can hardly deny that he, like other ancient writers, fails to conform to our principles of historiography. But the growth of a historical sense has made us less prone to pronounce judgment on writers of the past according to our standards without bearing in mind the nature of their own. Further, we have had good opportunities to study despotism at close quarters, and our experience

---

[1] See H.R. Trevor-Roper, *Gibbon* (1963), xvi.

has confirmed that Tacitus' depiction of its workings is less lacking in verisimilitude that many of our most comfortably situated predecessors have supposed. In recent years a reaction in Tacitus' favour has taken place. One of the most eminent historians of our own day broke new ground with a study of the Augustan Principate, so much idealised during the nineteenth century, from a Tacitean point of view, thereby throwing a brilliant new light on every corner of the subject.[2] Since then he has presented Tacitus himself, in a work of the greatest learning and intelligence, with sympathetic understanding. His Tacitus is shrewd, sceptical, unbiased, and wholly different from the sour, malignant slanderer others have depicted.

In the past Tacitus appeared to some as a cynic, to others as an idealist; to some as the counsellor of tyrants, to others as their enemy; to some as a judicious historian, to others as a malicious rhetorician. Since the rise of objective historical studies in the nineteenth century, we have been less prone to force ancient writers into taking sides in the controversies of our own time. But even nowadays Tacitus still provokes the most varying assessments and arouses the most diverse emotions. In the pages that follow we will inquire into the reasons.

Tacitus as a historian

The place of Tacitus among the world's greatest historians has been disputed, but few will challenge his claim to rank among its greatest writers. First, he is the creator of a style of unique power, dignity and appropriateness to the subject matter. Strict classicists will deplore it as they did in fifteenth-century Italy and in eighteenth-century France; for like his master, Sallust, Tacitus deliberately rejected the flowing, balanced periods of Ciceronian prose in favour of a harsh and abrupt structure suited to the severity of his matter. No way of writing could be more remote from that of common speech; his language and vocabulary are to a large degree archaic and poetical. Tacitus was the leading orator of his time, trained from boyhood to persuade an audience. His style is nothing if not rhetorical, deliberate, and artificial in the extreme. Tacitus' manner varies with his matter. Sometimes he is flowing, ornate and eloquent, notably in the *Agricola*, a work belonging to a genre halfway between oratory and history, and in the *Dialogue on Orators* where the style approaches that of the inventor of this kind of dialogue in Latin, Cicero. More often he is brief, swift, concise, concentrated to the utmost. He takes over from

[2] See above, pp. 74f.

his predecessors the traditional methods of annalistic history. Each year's events are grouped under the names of its two consuls; speeches – in most cases free compositions of the historian, skilfully varied according to speaker and occasion – are put into the mouths of characters at suitable moments; elaborate descriptive set pieces are frequently inserted. Yet Tacitus never degenerates into empty rhetoric; he is preserved from doing so by a truly Roman flair for the actual and the concrete, which fastens unerringly on the salient characteristics of a person or an episode. No historian draws more striking brief sketches of his characters – for instance, those of Poppaea Sabina (*Annals* XIII, 45) and Petronius (*Annals* XVI, 18); none has painted more impressively elaborate portraits than those of Nero, Agrippina, and above all Tiberius. No historian has surpassed him in descriptive power. Take for instance his narrations of the deaths of Galba and Vitellius – the latter all the better to be appreciated if one contrasts it with the matter-of-fact telling of the same story in Suetonius' life of that emperor (ch. 16f.); the Bacchanalian festival of Messallina; the suppression of Piso's conspiracy against Nero. No historian has equalled him in the power to coin epigrammatic sayings that are at once concise, striking and profound. Galba was '*omnium consensu capax imperii nisi imperasset*', ('by universal consent worthy of empire, till he ruled'); the brutal camp prefect Aufidienus Rufus, risen from the ranks, was '*eo immitior quia toleraverat*' ('all the more savage for having gone through the mill'); Domitian could not forgive Agricola because '*proprium humani ingenii est odisse quem laeseris*' ('it is part of human nature to hate those whom you have injured'). The list could be protracted indefinitely.

Tacitus' reputation as a writer needs no defence. But must we agree with the eminent German Latinist who at the close of the last century excused Tacitus' failings on the ground that he was not a historian, but a poet? To assess his qualities as a historian, we must consider first his principles and methods. First, it is necessary to understand his attitude to facts. The ancient world did not demand that a historian should himself labour to establish his facts with all possible certainty. If he was writing of his own times, he was obliged to undertake some measure of research; but otherwise he would closely follow written sources. Tacitus used the works of several predecessors, whom he sometimes mentions. We see from the first chapter of the *Annals*, that he held them in no high esteem. Their works are lost, but we can get some notion of how Tacitus used them by comparing his work with that of other writers who used the same material: with the Roman history written in Greek by the consul Cassius Dio during the third century and with the lives of emperors written by Plutarch in

Tacitus' own time and by Suetonius a little later. When Tacitus finds different stories of the same event he sometimes gives both, quoting the source for each by name; but on the whole he seems to have followed his predecessors in factual matters very closely. In some cases he made use of published speeches. The original of the speech of Claudius at Lyons given by Tacitus in his own version in *Annals* XI, 24 has been preserved in an inscription, and shows that while condensing and improving it, Tacitus was faithful to its general sense. Once only Tacitus quotes the archives of the Senate. How often he made use of them is a controversial question, but it seems unlikely that he did so frequently. Sometimes we can convict him of actual error. Some of his mistakes are trifling, like his confusion between the two daughters of Mark Antony or the two tribunes called Livius Drusus; more serious is the topographical mistake in the account of Otho's defeat at Bedriacum (*Histories* II, 40) and the apparent error in a point of constitutional history which a recently found inscription has exposed (*Annals* I, 15).

Tacitus cannot be accused of having taken no trouble to find out the truth; he took as many pains as most ancient historians. Like them, he was not a researcher in the modern sense; had he been so he would have run counter to the whole conception of history current in his time, and we cannot reasonably reproach him for his failure. Nor can we blame him for not having been interested in the same kind of facts that interest most modern historians. Tacitus shows very little concern and not much respect for the common man. He contributes little to our knowledge of the economic history of the period; and he tells us little of the provinces, except when war or rebellion breaks out in one of them. The mention of some Greek city with a famous past or of a nation with a curious history, like the Jews, stimulates him to antiquarian digression. His interests are the traditional interests of Roman annalists – the wars and victories of Rome and the history of her governing class. To many modern critics this point of view will seem narrow; and he omits much that to a modern historian would seem essential to his purpose. His conception of history was not the same as ours. It follows, not that he was necessarily a bad historian, but that he was a historian of a different kind from that which is now fashionable.

The charge of indifference to truth that is levelled against Tacitus gains more substance from his subtle and pervasive use of innuendo to present facts in such a manner that the reader puts the worst construction on the motives of certain of his characters. A person who has read the *Annals* casually or long ago would very likely believe that Tacitus actually stated that Germanicus was poisoned by Piso on the orders of Tiberius. That is not the case; but the narrative is artfully constructed so as to leave one with that impression. Again, the reader might well think that Tacitus actually reported that the great fire at Rome in Nero's reign was started by the Emperor. In fact Tacitus denies this allegation; but he has presented the episode in such a way that the reader is left with the impression that Nero's guilt is probable. Above all, Tacitus' whole presentation of Tiberius is coloured by this technique of innuendo. His considered view is that Tiberius became a tyrant only after the death of his son Drusus (*Annals* VI, 51). Yet like most ancient writers he ignores the possibility of change or development in character, and so must insist that the evil characteristics which Tiberius showed in later life must have been latent in his nature from the start. In keeping with this belief, he puts the worst possible construction on every act and saying of the Emperor, even when these acts and sayings are, to all appearance, exactly those of which we might expect the historian to approve. For the sake of contrast with his black portrait of Tiberius, Tacitus has idealised his adopted son, Germanicus, whose victories in Germany were clearly far less important than the narrative would lead us to suppose.

To judge Tacitus' attitude fairly, we must examine the reasons that led him to adopt it. Like his predecessors in writing Roman history, he avows an aim that is first and foremost moral. He will put on record good actions to be admired and bad actions to be despised, thus encouraging the former and discouraging the latter. Tacitus did not take this duty lightly. Livy had been unusual among Roman historians in being a private person outside politics. Most of the others held office in the Roman state; and Tacitus had been consul and had held the most important of Rome's provincial governorships. Tradition demanded that the historian should survey the actions he recorded from the standpoint of the austere antique *virtus* – the word means something between 'courage,' 'manliness,' and 'excellence' – supposed to have been universal among noble Romans in the early ages of the Republic's history. The golden age of Rome was located in the remote past. Recent history had for centuries been held to show a degeneration from this legendary ideal. We find this attitude in the enthusiastic Livy, strongly though he maintains that Augustus by his 'restoration of the Republic' and by his moral legislation has to a large extent revived the ancient virtues; we find it in the disillusioned Sallust, although what we know of Sallust's private character hardly suggests that he came nearer to the pattern of antique morality than did most Roman nobles of his day.

Tacitus' insistence on judging the men and actions of his own period by this exacting and somewhat superannuated standard must often strike an artificial note. In a year that had contained some of the most hideous cruelties perpetrated by Tiberius, one of the most grievous events, according to Tacitus, was the marriage of Julia, great-granddaughter of Augustus, to a man who though wealthy and respectable happened not to be a member of the Senate (*Annals* VI, 27). Livia, great-niece of Augustus and wife of Tiberius' son Drusus, 'polluted herself and her ancestors by adultery with a man from an Italian municipality.' The man in question was the prefect of the praetorian guard, Sejanus, at that time the most influential adviser of Tiberius. Nero's worst atrocities, including the murder of his mother, do not shock Tacitus more than his public appearances as a charioteer or a musician. Yet it is unlikely that Tacitus was himself a Roman of ancient lineage. Since his family probably came from Gallia Narbonensis, he was therefore further removed from the ancient aristocracy than either Rubellius Blandus, from Latium, or Aelius Sejanus, from Etruria.

One may make allowances for this attitude by suggesting that the holders of high office at all periods felt themselves to be members of a select body. But it is more relevant to observe that Tacitus is here expressing an attitude that was part of the tradition taken over from his predecessors. In the same way he will enumerate prodigies that have been thought to portend sinister events, and he will use the special knowledge gained as the holder of an important priesthood to expound the niceties of the official cult – niceties for which Tiberius and Domitian also had a special relish. A writer who continued the Roman tradition of annalistic history would almost inevitably approach his matter from the standpoint of the ancient aristocracy with its traditional attitudes and prejudices; and a writer of provincial origins – as, in all likelihood, Tacitus was – who had reached a high position in the Roman state would have been especially unlikely to form an exception to this rule.

This prejudice helps to determine an attitude to the Principate that is far from simple. The reader who starts from the beginning of the *Annals* will at first suppose that it is altogether hostile; but as he reads on he will revise his judgment. First, he will be surprised to find that Tacitus explicitly acknowledges that in the present state of the Empire and the world there is no alternative to monarchic government. What would happen without it can be inferred from the memory of the long period of civil war before Augustus, or from the events of 69 AD, the Year of the Four Emperors, after the extinction of the dynasty founded by Augustus had left the succession open, teaching the army commanders the 'secret of the Empire, that emperors could be made elsewhere than at Rome' (*Histories*, I, 4).

It might be argued that in thus acknowledging the necessity of the Principate, Tacitus was only paying lip service to the government which he was obliged to serve. We may therefore assess the sincerity of his profession by applying to it a test that is often useful in discovering the standpoint of a historian who gives no explicit statement of his own views and sympathies. Thucydides is notoriously such a case. Some have thought him a relentless enemy of the Athenian democracy from the start, others have supposed him a partisan of Pericles, and others have believed him first a friend and later an enemy of the demos. If we inquire which particular men and which forms of government Thucydides admires, we find that the Athenian whom, after Pericles, he especially praises is the moderate oligarch Antiphon, and that the government he thinks the best at Athens in his time is that of the Five Thousand, established by Antiphon and his friends in 411. Starting from this point of reference we find that Thucydides' other utterances are not hard to reconcile with the viewpoint which this explicitly stated attitude seems to presuppose.

Let us now apply the same test to Tacitus. Under Nero and the Flavian emperors an attitude of extreme opposition was bravely kept up by a small family group of senators, led first by Thrasea Paetus, then by his son-in-law, Helvidius Priscus, and lastly by Helvidius' son and namesake. They were sustained partly by their strict adherence to the dogmas of the Stoic sect, but even more by the example of heroes of the last phase of the Republic, like Brutus, Cassius, and the younger Cato, men who had chosen death rather than submission to the dictatorship of Julius Caesar. Tacitus handles these martyrs of republicanism with real sympathy and admiration, but by no means with unqualified approval. We first met Thrasea protesting in the Senate about a trivial matter, the affair of a gladiatorial show at Syracuse. Protests of this nature do no good, says Tacitus (*Annals* XIII, 49). Next, while the Senate is justifying Nero's murder of his mother by its sycophantic resolutions, Thrasea walks out, 'thereby imperilling himself', says Tacitus, 'without communicating to the other senators any impulse towards freedom' (*Annals* XIV, 12). Later, by a gallant effort, Thrasea saves from condemnation a man whose conduct would afterwards show that he had much better have been left to his fate (*Annals* XIV, 48-9; cf. XVI, 14). Similarly, in his character sketch of the elder Helvidius (*Histories* IV, 6), Tacitus records that some found that he cared too much for reputation.

The men Tacitus most admires are not these brave but ineffective martyrs of republicanism; they are the men who quietly carried on the business of the state, ignoring the injustices of a tyrannical emperor. The most obvious example is that of Tacitus' own father-in-law,

Julius Agricola, who did not allow the disappointment of his hopes of
employment to tempt him into treasonable activity against Domitian.
'Those who habitually admire illegal activity,' Tacitus writes, 'should
know that even under bad emperors there can be great men, and that
obedience and discretion, if combined with application and activity,
can raise a man to no less exalted heights than are reached by perilous
paths, with no advantage to the commonwealth beyond the fame won
by an ambitious death' (*Agricola* 42). In earlier times also it
is men like this whom Tacitus admires. Under Tiberius he singles out
for special praise two distinguished members of the ancient nobility,
Marcus Lepidus and Lucius Piso (*Annals* IV, 20; VI, 10). 'Lepidus,'
writes Tacitus, accentuating with an echo of Sallust the archaic
solemnity of his language, 'was for that age a wise and high-principled
man. Many a cruel suggestion made by the flattery of others he
changed for the better, and yet he did not want tact, seeing that he
always enjoyed a uniform prestige, and also the favour of Tiberius.'
Piso, he says, 'never proposed a servile motion, and, whenever
necessity was too strong for him, he would suggest judicious
compromises.' So too he commends Lucius Volusius, who died at
ninety-three under Nero, 'having used his great wealth to do good,
and having enjoyed the friendship of so many emperors without
having used it to do harm to others.' In Nero's reign he praises the
conduct of Memmius Regulus, whose 'prestige, loyalty, and
reputation made him, as far as the Emperor's overshadowing pre-
eminence allowed, truly distinguished.' Regulus had quietly resigned
his wife, Lollia Paulina, to the Emperor Gaius, had conveyed her to
him at Rome and presided over their betrothal. He, like others, was
notable for 'obedience and discretion'.

Above all, Tacitus is markedly sympathetic in his attitude to the
great writer and statesman whose career, more than any other,
illustrates the dilemma that confronted the leading Romans of those
times and whose character has since then been endlessly debated –
Marcus Annaeus Seneca. The son of a wealthy rhetorician who had
come to Rome from Corduba in Spain, Seneca early made his mark as
orator and man of letters. Under Claudius his career suffered a
setback: indiscreet familiarity with an imperial princess led to his
banishment to Corsica. But the Emperor's marriage with Agrippina,
the sister of Seneca's alleged mistress, more than restored his fortunes.
Agrippina chose him as Nero's tutor, and with his pupil's accession he
became, for the first few years of the new reign, the most influential
man in Rome. He accumulated vast wealth, often the subject of
hostile comment. According to one story, the revolt of Boudicca in
Britain was partly occasioned by his relentless usury. Yet for the most

part he used his influence over Nero to promote good government and to resist evil influences. For that Tacitus gives him full credit. His account of Seneca's last hours, when, ousted from the Emperor's favour by the intrigues of Tigellinus and Poppaea, he became implicated in Piso's conspiracy and received orders to commit suicide, is one of his most moving passages.

A final example serves perhaps best of all to illustrate the attitude of Tacitus. After the period of chaos that followed Nero's fall, some senators hoped that they might bring to book the notorious informers and prosecutors who had grown rich on the proceeds of Nero's reign of terror. Helvidius Priscus made the first move. The Senate was to send a congratulatory mission to the new Emperor, Vespasian, still absent in the East. The composition of such an embassy would normally be settled by drawing lots, but Helvidius proposed that on this occasion the magistrates should make a special selection. He calculated that the Neronian prosecutors would be excluded from the embassy and that their omission would be widely held to show that they were now discredited (*Histories* IV, 6 ff.). The proposal of Helvidius was opposed by one of the ablest and most unscrupulous of the informers, Eprius Marcellus. Why, Tacitus makes him argue, should the Senate depart from precedent? Any of its members will be able to attest its deference. The obstinacy of certain persons must not be allowed to provoke an emperor who would begin by carefully scrutinising each senator's looks and words. He, Marcellus, always remembered the nature of the times, the character of the constitution; he admired the institutions of the past, but followed those of the present; he prayed for good emperors, but put up with whatever emperors they had. It was not his speech, but the judgment of the Senate that had destroyed Thrasea. Nero's friendship toward him had brought him no less anxiety than exile had to others. In loyalty and courage Helvidius might be a second Cato. He, Marcellus, was simply one member of the Senate which like him had been enslaved to Nero. The historian's pervasive irony is directed against Marcellus, but not only against him. Can we really feel certain that the attitude ascribed to Helvidius is in all ways closer to Tacitus' own than that which he attributes to the archinformer?

Nothing that Tacitus said about the Julio-Claudian or the Flavian dynasty was likely to offend the regime under which he wrote. When he began his historical activity, the Julio-Claudian house had been extinct for thirty years; and the Flavian had lately ended with Domitian's murder, followed by the official condemnation of his memory. The new regime of Nerva and his successor, Trajan, did not in its actions depart so far from the policies of its predecessors as its

words might lead one to suppose; but by its official propaganda it
tried to dissociate itself from them as much as possible. We can see
this most easily from the panegyric on Trajan and the published
correspondence of Tacitus' friend and collaborator the younger Pliny.
But we see it also from other monuments of the time, and especially
from the satiric poetry of Martial and Juvenal. Some critics still
regard Juvenal as a courageous denouncer of contemporary abuses,
but in his first satire he announces that he will attack the dead, and he
keeps strictly to his programme.

Tacitus' tone of hostility toward earlier emperors is wholly in
keeping with this general tendency of the age in which he wrote; nor is
it inconsistent with his expressed belief that monarchic government is
in his time a necessity. In the *Agricola* (ch. 3) he warmly praises
Nerva and Trajan. Nerva, he says, has combined two things formerly
thought irreconcilable, liberty and the Principate. It has been
maintained that this praise is not sincere, that we cannot know
Tacitus' real sentiments towards these emperors since if they had
been hostile he could not have expressed them openly. It has even
been contended that his works convey a cryptic comment on the
happenings of the time after Domitian; that the account of Piso's
adoption by Galba in the first book of the *Histories* glances at Trajan's
adoption by Nerva; that the description of Nero's degrading
indulgence in Greek practices is meant as a warning to another
admirer of the Greeks, the Emperor Hadrian; and that Hadrian is
obliquely reproached for his abandonment of Trajan's policy of
conquest. But theories like these are mere speculations. Nothing in the
text compels belief in them, and we have seen that a study of the men
marked out by Tacitus for special admiration is decidedly opposed to
them. In his own public life he seems to have followed the course laid
down by Agricola: under Vespasian, Titus, and Domitian his career
prospered. A remarkable passage in the *Agricola* suggests that he was
driven to assert his principles all the more fervently by a secret sense of
guilt. Agricola was fortunate, he writes, in dying before Domitian's
reign of terror in 93, when a group of Stoic martyrs suffered death or
exile; he thereby escaped the guilt that attached to those who stood
helplessly by while the younger Helvidius and his friends met their
fate. '*Our* hands dragged Helvidius to prison; *we* were polluted by
looking on while Mauricus and Rusticus went to their ordeal; *we* were
stained with Senecio's innocent blood' (*Agricola*, ch. 45). Seen in the
light of these revealing words, Tacitus' repeated implication that men
like Agricola are more deserving of imitation than men like Thrasea
seems significant.

The profound ambiguity of Tacitus' attitude toward the principate lends to his writing an element of insincerity, with which his training as an advocate stands in close connection. But this very ambiguity helps him to throw light in innumerable ways upon the tensions and contradictions of his period. Throughout that time the government of the Empire was on the whole good and successful. The personal character of the emperor did not greatly affect the welfare of the provinces, which were in general much better off than they had been under the governors of the republican period, unaccountable to an emperor. No one can deny that Tacitus fails to give the principate full credit for these achievements; for not only his prejudice against the emperors of whom he writes, but also the restriction of his interests prevent him from doing them justice. But though a modern reader may deplore Tacitus' preoccupation with the relation of the emperors to the governing class at Rome, he can hardly contend that it is either uninteresting or unimportant. All ancient history – perhaps all history – is the history of a ruling oligarchy. To grasp its nature we must follow the changes in the composition of the governing class and the extent and distribution of its powers; and this Tacitus helps us to do. His conception of the history of the period as a personal drama played out between the emperors and the governing class does, in a sense, limit his sphere and narrow his sympathies. But at the same time it not only helps to invest his writing with its immense dramatic power, but gives him the opportunity to display an acute, if in some ways restricted, historical insight.

Many writers suppose that all great historians depend upon some particular philosophy or set of general principles. Some of these have reproached Tacitus with his deficiency in this respect, and others have been at pains to fill the gap with a set of principles of their own manufacture. Stoic elements in his thought may be discovered, as they may be discovered in the thought of any writer of his time. But his work yields no evidence whatever of an adherence to the tenets of any systematic philosophy, whether Stoic, Epicurean, or incipient Neoplatonist. Tacitus is wholly Roman in his lack of interest in general ideas. The nearest thing to a philosophy that can be discovered in his work is a somewhat vague belief in fate and destiny. Whether, like most educated as well as uneducated people in his time, he believed that what fate held in store for the future could be predicted has been a matter of dispute. In a famous passage (*Annals* VI, 22) he notices the Epicurean and Stoic attitudes toward prediction, and then declares that most men hold firmly that the future can be predicted, but that many of them fail to profit by accurate predictions through the false constructions placed upon them by those who make them. The belief ascribed by Tacitus to most men is not necessarily his own; but it must be noted that in two places he happens to report cases of just such misconstructions as this belief supposes. When Tiberius left Rome for Capri in 26 AD, the prediction that he would never return was widely reported. Some inferred that he would die soon and based their plans upon the inference. These people were disappointed, for the Emperor lived another eleven years without returning to the city (*Annals* IV, 58). The Jews were encouraged in their rash resistance to overwhelming power by a prophecy that people setting out from their country would gain the empire of the world. This prophecy, Tacitus tells us (*Histories* V, 13), referred not to the Jews, but to Vespasian and his son Titus. When Tacitus speaks disparagingly of Otho's reliance on his court astrologer or dryly observes that the predictions of Vespasian's future greatness were believed after the event, we cannot safely infer that he was exempt from a belief that in his time was almost universal. He speaks without disrespect of Tiberius' astrologer, Thrasyllus, who was also a philosopher of some distinction. And would the ultrasceptical Tacitus of some historians have found it necessary to observe that at the time of Otho's death people near Reggio di Emilia noted the appearance of a strange and peculiar-looking bird?

Tacitus may be reproached with bias and unfairness; with an indifference to truth, which he has in common with most ancient historians; with an element of insincerity closely bound up with his attitude to the principate, and with his lack of philosophical and religious principles. As an artist and as a historian he seizes the advantages that correspond to all these limitations. The very ambiguity of his attitude to Roman politics, together with his typically Roman feeling for the concrete and actual in any fact or situation, helps him again and again to do justice to the infinite complications and inconsistencies of real life. He can record a discreditable action of the virtuous Barea Soranus (*Annals* XXII, 53); he can give full credit to the excellence as a provincial governor of the infamous Lucius Vitellius (*Annals* VI, 32); he can keep in mind the weak points of Thrasea, Helvidius, and Seneca and the strong points of Suillius Rufus, Eprius Marcellus, and Vibius Crispus. Above all, he can achieve the marvellous chiaroscuro of his portrait of Tiberius. Despite the monstrous unfairness of many of the constructions which he puts upon this emperor's motives, despite the horror and disgust with which he describes his hideous cruelties, the reader cannot help suspecting that of all the characters in his history this is the one with whom Tacitus secretly has most in common. He sees the early period of imperial history as a tragic struggle between the emperors and the senatorial aristocracy, inevitable from the start and destined to prove fatal to both. A modern historian surveying the same field would not find this manner of approach congenial. Yet to Tacitus it offered unlimited opportunities not simply for the exercise of supreme literary art but for the attainment of profound though partial insight both into the history of the time that he recorded and into many permanent features of the human situation.

The Delphic Oracle

The ancient Greeks believed that the oracle at Delphi went back to immemorial antiquity. But were they right? The history of the site has been traced through excavations that are among the greatest achievements of modern archaeology. The interest of the French school in Delphi goes back to 1861, but for political reasons systematic excavation could not begin till 1893; since 1902 the series of volumes of the *Fouilles de Delphes* has appeared regularly. Mycenaean Delphi has been shown to have amounted to very little; and the chief centre seems to have been not on the site of the great temple, but at Marmaria, near the temple of Athene Pronaia. A few clay figurines may pertain to a private, but hardly to a public cult; an isolated Minoan marble drinking-horn shaped like a lion's head proves little. By the beginning of the Dark Age the settlement seems to have been destroyed by fire; before its life resumes during the Protogeometric period, there seems to have been a complete break in continuity. Only when the Dark Age is over does Delphi become important.

It is true that the mentions of Pytho in Homer suggest that the oracle was already celebrated. In the Catalogue of Ships it is simply one among several Phocian villages. But in the ninth book of the *Iliad* (404-5) Achilles declares that he would still reject Agamemnon's overtures, even if the king were to offer him all the wealth of Troy or Egyptian Thebes, or all that the stone threshold of the archer contains within it, in rocky Pytho. In the eighth book of the *Odyssey* (79f.) there is mention of a prophecy of Apollo, made to Agamemnon in glorious Pytho after he had crossed the stone floor to consult the god; this is the first mention of Delphi as a place of prophecy. Hesiod in his *Theogony* (498f.) says that Zeus placed at glorious Pytho, in the hollows of Parnassus, the great stone which his mother, Rhea, had given to her husband Kronos to swallow to prevent him from swallowing Zeus himself, as he had swallowed all their other children. Most people at present favour the eighth century as the time at which the epic poems

* This essay first appeared in *Greece and Rome* 23 (1976), 59-73.

reached their present form. If these passages are as early, it is surprising that they make Delphi seem as well established as they do.

The Greeks well knew that Apollo was a late comer to Delphi. The view that startled the learned world when Wilamowitz put it forward, that this god, the classical embodiment of the distinctively Hellenic qualities, entered Greece from Asia at a comparatively late date, has been confirmed by much evidence that was unknown when it was first expressed.[1] The French excavations at Delos – appropriately, France has taken in charge both the two greatest centres of Apollo's worship – have shown that the mother and daughter, in historical times called Leto and Artemis, were established on Delos well before Apollo; no wonder Apollo in the *Iliad* takes the Trojan side. The earliest Greek *so does Artemis* account of the coming of Apollo to Delphi is contained in the Delphian section of the Homeric Hymn to him, perhaps a work of the seventh century. In order to found his oracle by the Castalian Spring, Apollo has to kill a monstrous female serpent, who on Hera's orders has brought up Typhon, the most terrible of the enemies of Zeus. In the later-attested tradition, this serpent is male, and his significance is different. A legend first told by Euripides in a chorus of his *Iphigenia in Tauris* (1234f.), but found in many later texts, says that the serpent was Python, the holy serpent of the Earth Goddess, Gaia, to whom the oracle belonged before Apollo's coming. We must be careful to call him Python and not *the* Python, for feat of incurring the wrath of Professor Joseph Fontenrose, who in an exhaustive monograph[2] has written his biography and linked him with countless other mythical monsters. The Python story must be much older than Euripides. Aeschylus in the prologue of his *Eumenides* offers what is clearly a censored version of the story, in which Gaia gives the oracle to Themis, Themis to the Titaness Phoebe, and Phoebe makes it a birthday present to her grandson Apollo. Aeschylus must have avoided the story of Apollo's violent conquest of the shrine. Many scholars have argued that the Python story must be earlier than the legend told in the Homeric Hymn. This is by no means certain. Delphi had to struggle for primacy against an oracle whose claim to be the most ancient was perhaps more convincing than her own; an oracle, moreover, which claimed to derive its prophecies from Zeus

---

[1] But W. Burkert, *Rheinisches Museum* 118 (1975), 1f., has now made a strong case for connecting Apollo's name with 'ἀπελλα, the word for the assembly of adult males, and has argued that he originated in the Peloponnese. He has also (in *Grazer Beiträge* 4, 1975, 51f.) pointed out that Greek archaic statues of Apollo continue an Oriental type common since the second millennium B.C. The Apollo of historical times may well contain elements of different origin.

[2] *Python* (Berkeley 1959).

himself – the great oracle of Dodona, in Epirus to the far north. Delphi countered Dodona's claim to be authorised by Zeus by insisting that Apollo derived his omniscience from Zeus his father. To counter Dodona's claim of greater antiquity, she had to assert the continuity of Apollo's oracle with an ancient oracle on the same site that had belonged to Gaia. But was there really such an ancient oracle? The archaeological evidence alone hardly suggests it. Perhaps the serpent killed by Apollo was originally simply the guardian of the sacred spring, like the dragon killed by Cadmus when he founded Thebes; perhaps it was only later that this dragon became Python. In the Hymn the dragon is female, doubtless because the story of the shrine belonging to Gaia had somehow led to the serpent being confused with the goddess herself and taking on her gender. But that does not prove the legend earlier than the seventh century. The Hymn claims that the Delphians were descended from Cretan sailors who had been trying to make for Pylos, but were diverted to Pytho by the god. This has been connected with the discovery of Cretan objects among the eighth- and seventh-century finds at Delphi; it may indicate an early connection between Delphi and Dorian Crete, where the cult of Apollo flourished.

Delphi had over Dodona the advantage of a more central position and better communications both by land and sea. From the late eighth century on we have evidence that it was consulted by various Greek communities, notably by Corinth and Sparta, but also by towns in Achaea, in the northern Peloponnese, and even by cities in Euboea. W.G. Forrest argues[3] that in the famous war of the late eighth century which began over the rich Lelantine Plain in Euboea, but then spread over the Greek world, Delphi was a partisan of Chalcis and her allies against Eretria and others. The friends of Chalcis lay near Delphi; Corinth, Thessaly, and Sparta were all near at hand. The mere facts of geography are enough to show why these states are prominent among early consulters of the oracle. One of Eretria's allies, Miletus, had its own great Apolline oracle at Branchidae, and hardly needed Delphi. Yet from the early seventh century the oracle came to be consulted by islanders: Paros, Thera, and Rhodes all figure among inquirers.

Both individuals and whole communities could ask Apollo for advice about practical problems and about what results would follow a particular course of action. Many of the early recorded consultations deal with the founding of colonies. When a new colony was being planned, the intending founders would consult the oracle and would

[3] *Historia* 6 (1957), 160-75; but see now D. Fehling, *Rheinisches Museum* 122 (1979), 199f.

seek the encouragement of a favourable response. During the eighth century all the colonies known to have been associated with Delphi were in Sicily or southern Italy; then in the seventh there are colonies in Thrace to the north and in Africa to the south. It has been argued that Delphi provided the main impetus for the colonising movement, and that its priests maintained a vast archive of information that would be useful to intending colonisers. This, I think, is a mistaken view, rightly rejected by the leading modern authority on the oracle, H.W. Parke. Parke's history of the oracle, first published in 1939, came out in 1956 in a second edition written with the help of his colleague D.E.W. Wormell.[4] The volume containing the actual history is accompanied by a second volume containing the evidence for all recorded responses of the oracle, both certain and dubious. He believes that the initiative for a new colony, and also the bulk of the information needed, was supplied by the intending colonisers; he illustrates his view of the way things happened from the well-known instances of the oracles given to Archias, the Corinthian founder of Syracuse in 734, and to Battus, the founder of Cyrene about a century later.[5]

Another important feature of the oracle's activity that can be traced back to the seventh century was that of regulating problems, and most particularly those regarding purification and blood-guilt. Although these concepts are not often mentioned in Homer, I am convinced that they were important long before his time, and they continued to be so till well into the fifth century. The myths of the matricidal heroes Orestes and Alcmaeon indicate their significance; both seem to have taken their present form during the seventh century, when Delphi provided the Greeks with authoritative guidance on such matters.

The shrine now began to receive precious offerings from great kings and rulers. Her connection with the wealthy power of Corinth, already strong under the rule of the aristocratic family called the Bacchiads, became still stronger under the great tyrant Cypselus. He came to power about the middle of the seventh century, and was the first donor to build a special treasury at Delphi to house his offerings. Delphi had a close link with Sparta and its royal houses. The kings based some of their claims upon a Delphic oracle, and they were attended by special officials called Pythioi, who managed their

---

[4] *A History of the Delphic Oracle* (Oxford); Parke followed this in 1967 with an excellent short book, *Greek Oracles* (London), available as a paperback in the Hutchinson University Library series. *The Delphic Oracle* by Joseph Fontenrose (1978), is learned but over-sceptical.

[5] On the myth of the early temples, see C. Sourvinou-Inwood, *CQ* 29 (1979) 231f.

relations with Delphi. The reforms attributed to Lycurgus derived much of their authority from being sanctioned by Delphi; it became the custom for new legal codes to be submitted to Apollo for his approval. When soon after the beginning of the sixth century the Delphians had to defend their control of the oracle against the powerful city of Crisa situated at the head of the gulf of Itea, they were able to invoke powerful foreign support. The Amphictyonic League had originally centred upon the temple of Demeter at Anthela near Thermopylae; it now made Delphi its centre and gave the oracle its protection. The Thessalian dynasts seem to have taken the lead in the so-called First Sacred War; but Cleisthenes, the famous tyrant of Sicyon, and Solon, another lawgiver who set store by Delphic sanction, both led contingents of their countrymen to help the Delphians. Athens had developed a strong Delphian connection at this time. Apollo as father of Ion, the mythical ancestor of the Ionian Greeks, acquired the title of the 'paternal god' of Athens, and special officials were appointed to give rulings in religious matters in close conjunction with the oracle.

Foreign rulers also sought Apollo's favour. The date and occasion of the alleged consultation by Midas, king of Phrygia, are uncertain, though Herodotus saw at Delphi a throne said to have been dedicated by him. But the Lydian kings Gyges, Alyattes, and Croesus certainly inquired at Delphi and made splendid offerings. The greatest of all the benefactors of the oracle was Croesus; he hoped for encouragement for the expedition against Persia he was planning partly, no doubt, because he was trying to obtain Spartan aid. Apollo's famous prediction to Croesus that if he crossed the Halys he would destroy a great empire looks very like an afterthought to replace a favourable response that after the event was better forgotten. The poet Bacchylides (3.75f.) wrote that Croesus was carried by Apollo to the land of the Hyperboreans and there lived happily ever after; oriental sources indicate that his life was not spared.

By the time of the great fire of 548 BC, the wealth of Delphi must have been by contemporary standards very great. We get a notion of the art of that time at Delphi from the sculptures of the Sicyonian Treasury. A vast subscription was launched to pay for the rebuilding of the temple; one of the most generous subscribers was Amasis, king of Egypt, who relied heavily on Greek mercenaries. In the final stages the great Athenian family of the Alcmaeonidae, then in exile during the rule of their enemies the Pisistratids, took over the building contract. In legend this was the fifth temple, in fact the second. The first was built of Apolline bay from the Vale of Tempe, where it grew in abundance in ancient times; the second was made by bees from beeswax and feathers, and was finally blown by a mighty wind to the land of the Hyperboreans, where Apollo used to spend the winter months. The third temple was built by Hephaestus and Athene; it had walls and pillars of bronze, and above the pediment sang golden Keledones, creatures like the Sirens. So sweet was their song that visitors to the temple forgot their homes and families and stayed to listen to it for ever, so that in the end Zeus and Poseidon had to destroy the temple with lightning and earthquake. The fourth temple, the one destroyed in 548, was attributed to the heroes Trophonius and Agamedes; Trophonius had his own oracle at Lebadeia in Boeotia, on the present road from Athens to Delphi, where in the neighbourhood of an awe-inspiring chasm the inquirer had to climb into a narrow hole in the ground and then had the impression of being swept away into the darkness. The new fifth temple was of marble, and the Alcmaeonids marked their gratitude to the god for having rewarded their piety by bringing them back from exile by setting a marble pediment over the front instead of the limestone one specified in the contract. We can get a notion of the splendour of the Alcmaeonid temple, and also of the formidable difficulties involved in building on this site from the magnificent supporting wall which survives from it.

Over the three entrances of the temple were inscribed three famous maxims: 'Nothing in excess', 'Know thyself' – which means not 'Practise introspection', but 'Remember that you are mortal' – and 'Go bail and ruin is at hand'. These maxims were associated with the sixth-century sages known as the Seven Wise Men; but the kind of wisdom they exemplify was ancient long before their time. It has been held to be specifically connected with Apollo, and Apollo is indeed the incarnation of the attitude to life which they exemplify. But this attitude is by no means exclusively Apolline, but rather common to the Greeks of epic and archaic times. Jean Defradas[6] is one of many who have believed in a specific Apolline wisdom, invented and preached to the Greeks at large by a powerful body of Delphian 'clergy'. This belief is false, as Defradas's distinguished countryman Pierre Amandry pointed out in a masterly review of his book.[7] The mountain villagers no more set themselves up as a clergy to preach a doctrine than they organised a vast information bureau for the benefit of intending colonisers and of a Panhellenic drive in search of *Lebensraum*. Their aim was to help Apollo to fulfil his promise to give advice to those who sought it, and in doing so to maintain the splendour of the sanctuary and to keep out of trouble.

[6] *Les Thèmes de la propagande delphique* (Paris 1954).
[7] *Revue de philologie* 30 (1956), 268-82.

The actual working of the oracle presents difficult and complex problems. The ancient evidence is surprisingly defective, and it is unlikely that general agreement on all the controversial issues will ever be attained. But the understanding of the question has been greatly furthered by Pierre Amandry;[8] the best modern treatment of the problem of the Pythia's trance is that of E.R. Dodds.[9]

The Pythia, the priestess of Apollo, was chosen from the local community. She had to be over fifty years of age, and was not permitted to indulge in sexual intercourse. The gender of a priest or priestess was normally the same as that of the divinity he served, and this exception to the rule must be accounted for. Rohde in his great
> book *Psyche*, published in the nineties of the last century, put it down to the influence of Dionysus, who was believed to take over Delphi during the winter months of Apollo's absence. But there is no evidence for Dionysus at Delphi earlier than the fifth century; and Rohde's theory depends on a distinction between Apollinian and Dionysiac prophecy rooted not in fact but in the theory of his early friend, Friedrich Nietzsche. In 1940 Kurt Latte suggested that the Pythia was a priestess of an oriental type who was imagined to be the consort of the god; he found this exemplified in the cult of Apollo at Patara in Lycia, and in the myth of Cassandra. He thought Apollo had brought the Pythia with him when he came from Asia. But there is no indication that the Pythia was ever imagined as being the consort of the god, and the cult of Patara is too different from that of Delphi to permit the drawing of analogies. More probably the priestess of the Earth Goddess had been female, and the gender of the priestess remained unchanged after its taking over by Apollo.

Originally consultations took place only on one day of the year, the seventh of the Delphic month Bysios, which was Apollo's birthday; this month corresponded with the second half of February and the first half of March. Later they were held on the seventh of every month, except for the three winter months of Apollo's absence. People who wanted advice at other times had to remain content with the oracle conducted by drawing lots in the shape of beans to determine answers to alternative questions. On the days of consultation there was a large crowd and a very long queue; in Plutarch's time there were two Pythias with a third in reserve, working in shifts.

At dawn the Pythia purified herself, and after testing the omens the priest sacrificed a goat, probably on the great altar east of the temple dedicated during the fifth century by the people of Chios. Then the

[8] *La Mantique apollinienne à Delphes* (Paris 1950).
[9] *The Greeks and the Irrational* (Berkeley 1951), 70ff.

Pythia entered the sanctuary and took her seat upon the god's sacred tripod. The priests and the inquirers also purified themselves with water from the Castalian spring, and the order of consultation was determined. It was fixed partly by lot and partly by precedence; the Delphians used to reward benefactors of their community by grants of priority in the consultation of the oracle. Consultation was of course free of charge, but the inquirer could not enter the temple till he had offered on the altar outside the sacred cake, and these cakes cost a great deal of money. There was a means test; communities paid more than individuals, and both communities and individuals paid according to their means. Then the consultant had to sacrifice sheep or goats on the inner hearth of the cella of the temple. In early times the Delphians were notorious for the greed with which they seized upon their portion of these sacrifices. It was in a dispute over sacrificial meat, according to Pindar in the *Sixth Paean*, that the hero Neoptolemus met his end. His shrine stands just outside the precinct, just as the shrine of Erechtheus stood on the Athenian Acropolis near Athena's temple and the shrine of Pelops at Olympia near the temples of Hera and of Zeus; probably he was brought by the northerners when they came to Delphi.

After the sacrifice the inquirer entered the inner sanctuary at the back of the temple. He sat in silence at the back of the room. The Pythia, already in a state of trance, was out of sight somewhere at the other end; either she was on a lower level or a curtain hid her. The inquirer was accompanied by the Prophetes, the chief priest, to whom he had already given his question, either verbally or in writing; the Prophetes now put it to the Pythia and received her answer. Her reply was shouted, and no doubt sounded incoherent; the Prophetes had to make sense of it and render it in hexameter verse. The rapid improvisation of hexameters is less difficult than some people imagine; it is helped by practice. These hexameters had a conventional style, based on that of epic verse, with formulaic phrases, ornate diction, and riddling paraphrases. After receiving the answer, the inquirer left the temple.

How was the Pythia induced to become the mouthpiece of Apollo? How was an elderly peasant-woman from a mountain village made to enter a trance and to emit prophetic ravings? Nineteenth-century rationalism produced a variety of ingenious answers, based upon this or that fragment of the ancient evidence. The tripod was supposed to have been placed over a deep chasm in the rock, from which mephitic vapours rose, inducing trance. But the archaeologists showed that there was no chasm, and the doctors showed that, if there had been, vapours rising from it could not have produced the supposed effect.

The Pythia is said to have chewed leaves of Apolline bay, and it was suggested that this caused her ecstasy; but Professor Oesterreich chewed large numbers of bay leaves, and found that he was no more inspired than usual. Most people now incline towards a psychological explanation; if you tell an elderly peasant woman that on a certain day and at a certain time she will become the mouthpiece of Apollo, you do not need to be a hypnotist to get the desired result. Dodds used extensive evidence from the observation of modern mediums to argue that the Pythia's trance must have been auto-suggestively induced.

It is not difficult for a rationalist of the nineteenth-century type to write off the procedure as manifest fraud. How could the Prophetes discharge his role without being aware that he was putting a response into the mouth of the god? But once more modern research into the psychology of religious belief, not to mention common sense, enjoins caution. The Prophetes knew, as all believers in the ancient gods knew, that gods commonly worked through men. Apollo worked not only through the Pythia, but through the Prophetes, who can scarcely have thought of his own action as a fraud. The members of the village community who served as priests accumulated in the course of centuries great experience. They must be given credit for much good sense, as a study of the responses collected by Parke and Wormell, with due allowance made for the presence of many prophecies made after the event and other doubtful items, will make clear. The advice given to inquirers is not only eminently practical; it is also based on sound moral and religious principles. Few individual consultants can have had occasion to reproach the god. Inquiries from communities or from their rulers about important public matters raised obvious difficulties. Anti-clerical critics can easily accuse the Delphians of cynical pursuit of their own private interest. They can point to some manifestly awkward incidents, like the alleged bribery that at the beginning of the fifth century secured the deposition of a king of Sparta, Demaratus, and led to the dismissal of the Pythia and the exile of a leading Delphian priest. They can accuse the Delphians of having supported the Lydians and later the Persians in their designs against Greek independence, or the Corinthians in the Lelantine War, or the Peloponnesians in their wars with Athens. But such accusations take into account only part of the complicated truth. Obviously Apollo wished to content everyone; obviously he gave the answer that would content most people, and at the same time protect the interests of his sanctuary. One may instructively compare the awkward position in which the Pope found himself during the war of 1939-45. Perhaps Pius XII was too careful of the interests of his Church at the expense of wider interests. But will anyone who is not hopelessly prejudiced contend that he really sympathised with Hitler or with Mussolini? The Delphians are a good deal easier to excuse, for before the Persian War Greek nationalism hardly existed, and Apollo was not a merely national god. Nor did the Lydians or the Persians subscribe to an ideology which Apollo's worshippers were bound to consider wicked.

The Persian invasion of 480 exposed the oracle to a severe test. The Delphians were well aware of the immense power of Persia, and were understandably reluctant to offend it. Before the revolt of the Ionian Greeks at the beginning of the century, the men of Cnidus in Caria had asked Apollo if they should make their city into an island by cutting a canal, obviously in order to hold out against Persian attack if necessary (Hdt. 1.174.4). The god answered that Zeus would have made their territory an island, had he wished to; clearly he did not wish to encourage a rebellion. When in 480 the Athenians asked Apollo what they should do in face of imminent invasion, they received this answer:

Wretches, why are you sitting there? Leave your homes and the hilltops of your wheel-shaped city and flee to the ends of the earth! Neither your head nor your body shall remain, nor your feet nor your hands nor any of your middle. Your state is not to be envied; you are struck down by fire and the fierce war god, driving on his Syrian chariot. He shall ruin many another fortress, and not yours alone; and he shall give many temples of the immortals to the ruthless fire. They now stand bathed in sweat, quivering with terror, and blood pours over their rooftops, as they foresee the compulsion of distress. Leave the temple, and let your thoughts dwell on trouble (Hdt. 7.140.1).

The Athenian envoys were greatly distressed at this answer; and an influential Delphian called Timon advised them to return as suppliants and to ask for a second answer. They took his advice, and told the god that if he did not offer a more encouraging response they would remain in the temple till they expired. That would have polluted the sanctuary; the same threat is used by the Danaids in Aeschylus' *Suppliants* to force the king of Argos to grant them protection. Apollo told them that Athena could not persuade Zeus to spare them, but that he would grant her that, though all of Attica was ruined, a wooden wall should remain, and should protect her and her children. They should not await the coming of an army, but should retire. 'Divine Salamis', the oracle concluded, 'you shall destroy the children of women, either when Demeter – the corn goddess – is being scattered or when she comes together.' Salamis was the obvious place for the Athenians to put their non-combatants.

It seems that the advancing Persians left Delphi alone. A story of how a force tried to attack it, but was destroyed through a miraculous agency, looks like an afterthought. After the battle of Salamis, Apollo seems to have changed his mind, for Plutarch (*Vita Aristidis* 11. 3) says that an inquiry by Aristides not long before the battle of Plataea provoked the response that if they prayed to certain specified gods the Athenians would be victorious. After the war Delphi was so far from having lost prestige that it received magnificent offerings from the Greek cities in honour of the victory. Marathon had already been commemorated by the erection of the Athenian Treasury, and now the Athenian Stoa commemorated Salamis and the states victorious at Plataea set up the golden tripod that bore the serpent column still to be seen in the Hippodrome in Constantinople. It was even proposed to dedicate to Apollo a tithe of the property of those Greek cities which had sided with the enemy, though the proposal was not adopted. To the same period belong the splendid dedications by which the Sicilian tyrants commemorated their victories over the Carthaginians and Etruscans and their successes in the great games, whose chief survival is the charioteer from the group dedicated by the brother of Gelon and Hieron, Polyzalus.

During the next half-century Delphi continued to be consulted by the principal Greek states, including Athens; Apollo blessed the transfer of the bones of Theseus from Scyros and the founding of the Italian colony of Thurii. But during the Peloponnesian War geography made it hard for Delphi to be neutral. When in 431 the Spartans asked Delphi whether they should go to war, he encouraged them and promised them his help, so that when the plague broke out at Athens people might remember the plague in the Greek camp started by Apollo's arrows in the first book of the *Iliad*. During the war the Athenians are known to have consulted Dodona and even the distant oracle of Zeus Ammon in the oasis of Siwa in the Libyan Desert; access to Delphi was in any case scarcely possible. Delphi received dedications for the Syracusan victory over Athens, and for Lysander's final victory at Aegospotami. Yet she seems to have done what she could to remain the common sanctuary of all Greeks. Both in 456 and again in 414 Argos, the ally of Athens, commemorated a victory over her hereditary enemies, the Spartans, with a Delphic dedication. The former was probably made during the short period of Phocian control over the oracle that followed the Athenian conquest of Boeotia at the battle of Oenophyta, and so may not be relevant; the second is a fact of special interest.

Sparta continued to be the most influential Greek community at Delphi till in 371 her defeat by the Thebans at Leuctra changed the balance of power. Two years before that, the Alcmaeonid temple had been ruined by an earthquake; ancient authors say surprisingly little about this event, but the inscribed building accounts reveal what happened. Again a vast subscription was opened; but before the work of restoration was complete a new disaster supervened. Under pressure in their war against the Thebans, the Phocians seized the sanctuary and plundered its treasures to pay their mercenary troops. Philip of Macedon got himself made president of the Amphictyonic League, and skilfully exploited the indignation which the sacrilege aroused; the Phocian defeat in the Third Sacred War of 346 was greatly to his advantage.

In the following years Athens preferred to consult Dodona; Demosthenes, if we may trust his enemy Aeschines, openly accused the Pythia of philippising. Philip and his son Alexander after him treated Delphi with respect, and in 330 the restoration of the temple was completed. But there is no indication that they thought the oracle politically important, and in the new world dominated by military monarchies Delphi could hardly hope to exercise the same influence that it had wielded in the old world of small city states. It still gave rulings in matters relating to religion, and it was still treated with general respect; but in high politics it no longer counted. In the closing years of the fourth century Demetrius Poliorcetes when he gained control of Athens did not only receive the divine honours of celebration in a paean and approach by an embassy whose members were styled not *presbeis* but *theoroi*; a decree echoing those referring to oracular responses ordained that his pronouncements should have the force of oracles. Even fifty years earlier, no such thing would have been possible.

Soon after the beginning of the third century, Delphi came to be dominated by the Aetolian League, the least civilized of the various forces that counted for something in the war and politics of the Hellenistic world. That domination lasted for about a century, until the Romans removed the Amphictyonic League from Aetolian control. A raid by the invading Gauls under Brennus in 279 was defeated, it appears, by an Aetolian and Phocian force, and the Aetolians spread stories of miraculous protection of the shrine calculated to boost their own reputation for piety. Many inscriptions found near the sanctuary name people whom they singled out for honour. Under their control the oracle continued to function, but hardly enjoyed its old prestige.

The Roman connection with Delphi goes back to the fourth century BC when the Romans, who had been preceded by the Etruscan city of Caere, or Agylla, rewarded Apollo for his share in the overthrow of

Veii by dedicating a golden mixing-bowl. In the crisis of the Second Punic War they sent Q. Fabius Pictor, the first Roman annalist, to consult the oracle, and he received a list of divinities to whom supplication should be made. During the period of extreme alarm that followed Cannae the government must have wanted to satisfy the people that every possible religious measure was being taken; but the move may indicate a wish for friendly relations with the Aetolians, and soon after Rome became their ally against Philip V of Macedonia. After the Metaurus, Delphi received a handsome offering; and when the Sibylline Books were found to have advised the bringing of the image of the Mother of the Gods from her shrine at Pessinus to Rome, Delphi took part in the transaction. But once Rome had gained the desired foothold in Greek politics, Delphi ceased to be consulted. The Romans had their own methods of divination, and the advice of Greek oracles was not needed.

The decline of Greek religion which had marked the Hellenistic age continued during the period of Roman domination. The educated classes showed respect to the old gods, but drew their real spiritual sustenance from philosophy, and the ignorant relied upon astrology and other superstitions of eastern origin: the ancient gods were still deferred to, but they were not worshipped with the old devotion. The philhellenic emperor Hadrian twice visited Delphi, and held the local archonship; in his time Herodes Atticus restored the stadium, and Plutarch took special pride in being a Delphic priest. Several of his works are concerned with Delphi, and tell us much about its history; and his connection with Delphi was an important element in the blend of ancient piety and more modern philosophy that make his work and personality so attractive.[10] But even Plutarch cannot conceal from himself the oracle's decline. He is clearly a little saddened by the oracle's responses being no longer given in verse. But in the peaceful conditions of his own age, he argues, there is less need for oracles in verse: 'War has ceased, migrations and civil strife exist no more, nor tyrannies, nor the other diseases and plagues of Greece, which needed the resources of many and powerful medicines.' Inquiries on trivial subjects, he believes, do not deserve poetic treatment. When Hadrian himself consulted Apollo, he did not ask him about affairs of state, but asked instead where Homer came from and who were his parents; Apollo answered that his country was Ithaca, and his parents Telemachus and Nestor's daughter Epicaste.

Within a century after Hadrian's time, the oracle seems to have become virtually silent. Christianity was now powerful, and it was

---

[10] It is well described by D.A. Russell, *Plutarch* (London 1972).

actively hostile to the pagan oracles; since it did not deny their effectiveness, it was obliged to attribute it to the agency of demons. A legend grew that these demons had abandoned their sanctuaries on the birth of Christ; and Eusebius, the panegyrist of Constantine the Great, speaks of a Delphic response given to Augustus which caused him to dedicate on the Capitol an altar 'to the first-born God'. Even under Constantine Delphi seems to have enjoyed some consideration; although Constantine looted its treasures to adorn his new capital, statues of him and his relations were still erected there. The last defender of the old religion, Julian, is said to have consulted Delphi, with other ancient oracles, before his fatal expedition to the East in AD 362. There is a tradition that Julian's quaestor, the great doctor Oreibasius, inquired of the oracle and received the following response: 'Tell the monarch, the marvellous court has fallen to the ground; no more does Phoebus occupy his house, no more his prophetic bay, no more his speaking fountain; even the talking water is cut off.'[11] The tradition cannot be believed. Little more than thirty years after Julian's death, Greece was brutally devastated by the barbarian horde of Alaric the Goth. According to Eunapius, the Goths were assisted in the work of destruction by Christian monks. It is easier now than it was a few years ago to imagine these, barefooted, covered with hair, stinking with the odour of sanctity and eagerly destroying the treasures of centuries in the name of their own sacred dogmas and emotions. Delphi must have been among the first objects of attack, and we can still observe the thoroughness with which the work was done. The imperial throne was then occupied by the bigot Theodosius, who had saved what could be saved of Roman fortunes after the disastrous defeat of Adrianople in 378. He issued orders that the material got from the destruction of temples should be used to repair roads, bridges, aqueducts, and walls. We can hardly doubt that it was after this event that the famous oracle said to have been given to Oreibasius came into being; it smacks too strongly of Christian propaganda to be genuine.[11] Now began the long centuries of the shrine's desertion.

---

[11] See C.M. Bowra, *On Greek Margins* (Oxford 1970), 233ff.

Index

112 plot over character
75 Aug. as successor to Pompey

62 Utopias
163 Fate & prediction (Tac. A. 6.22) -- Thrasyllus' son   [T. 146-65]
164 Thrasyllus.
41 American philistinism
166-79 Delphic o.